FLYING LIVES

with a

Norfolk Theme

by

Peter B. Gunn

Printers: Newprint and Design Ltd, Garrood Drive, Industrial Estate, Fakenham, Norfolk NR21 8NN

Front Cover painting: A formation of the aircraft of Sir Alan Cobham's Flying Circus in the early 1930s. (Reproduced from *Aeromodeller* December 1949: artist C. Rupert Moore)

ISBN: 978-0-9542770-1-7

Peter Gunn is a professional indexer and historian with a particular interest in airfield and aviation history. The author of four previous books, he lives in Docking with his wife Janet.

By the same author:
RAF Great Massingham: A Norfolk Airfield at War 1940-1945 (1990)
Airfield Focus (5): Bircham Newton (GMS Enterprises 1992)
Bircham Newton: A Norfolk Airfield in War and Peace (2002)
Naught Escapes Us: The Story of No. 206 Squadron Royal Air Force (The 206 Squadron Association 2004)

Dedicated to the family with a special mention for Eleni and Thanos

FLYING LIVES with a Norfolk Theme

CONTENTS

FOREWORD
by
Steve Snelling, former Eastern Daily Press Sunday editor

When it comes to charting the charismatic lives and trailblazing times of a few of the many heroic and occasionally hapless aeronauts who have taken to the skies over Norfolk, the inevitable difficulty is one of selection: who to pursue on that often erratic but always fascinating flightpath through history and who to ignore, or perhaps leave for another time-travelling aeronautical odyssey.

Such indeed is the seemingly inexhaustible supply of likely candidates, ranging from the pioneering 'balloonatics' to the great airshipmen of the inter-war years and from the daredevil adventurers of the early 20th century to their jet age successors, that when Peter Gunn first outlined his plans for this book I couldn't help but feel a pang of sympathy at the unenviable task he had set himself.

But I have to say he has proven himself more than equal to the challenge. His choice may not concur precisely with my own mind's-eye selection - I suspect I would have found it nigh impossible not to include one of Norfolk's favourite pre-1914 flying visitors, Bentfield Hucks - but it does follow a remarkably similar trajectory, featuring many of the notable and notorious characters who would undoubtedly rank high in any list I might seek to draw up; from the brave if wayward Major Money to Norfolk's Zepp hunter *par excellence* Egbert Cadbury and on to the legendary 007 flying double Ken Wallis.

Over the course of the last 35 years I have been fortunate enough to enjoy myriad journalistic encounters with these extraordinary aeronauts through interviews or research for articles that have appeared in the Eastern Daily Press, and it is an absolute pleasure to renew acquaintance with them via Peter's latest foray into Norfolk's aviation history.

To read Flying Lives is to revel in a veritable cornucopia of gripping yarns, from the tragic and gallant saga of the brothers Darley to the thrills and spills of Cobham's flying circus and the spectacular career of a true-life big screen hero. Some of these tales will, at least in part, be familiar to aviation enthusiasts, though Peter has worked tirelessly to shine fresh light on many of them, but other stories will, I fancy, be entirely new to all but a few. And of these, I was particularly captivated by the exploits of pioneering marine aviator Charles Herbert Collet, of whom I knew a little but not half as much as I do now having read Peter's enthralling entry, and of Lawrence Edwards' unfortunate claim to fame as the first officer PoW during the Second World War.

As might be expected of any project undertaken by Peter Gunn, Flying Lives is a thoroughly rewarding read, as rich in detail as it is alive with colourful anecdote, and does full justice to those pioneer balloonists and all those other magnificent men in their flying machines who left an indelible impression on this county's proud aviation history.

Steve Snelling,
Thorpe St Andrew, October, 2010.

INTRODUCTION and ACKNOWLEDGEMENTS

Flying Lives with a Norfolk Theme is the outcome of research for some of my earlier books about aviation history. As the work progressed I encountered many outstanding aviators from the earliest days of flight whose own stories deserved to be told. I use the term 'aviators' in its broadest sense to include aircrew, engineers and designers and have made a personal choice of a few whose stories are of particular interest or who in some cases have not always received their due recognition.

I make no claim for this book to be a comprehensive account of aviation in Norfolk. I hope that will not prove disappointing to those who feel that many famous names are not included. Perhaps a challenge for me in a future book?

My hope is that the book offers an insight into the lives of some of the personalities who took to the skies both in peace and war and of the others who made it possible.

I am grateful to the following organisations for their assistance in my research and for permission to use copyright material. These include the Imperial War Museum, the British Library, the National Archives in Kew and the Vickers Archives held at the Cambridge University Library, in particular John Wells and Don Manning. The Norfolk Record Office, the Norfolk Heritage Centre and the Norfolk & Norwich Millennium Library were useful sources. Mr Peter Elliott and the staff of the Royal Air Force Museum Reading Room at Hendon supplied me with much assistance. The National Monuments Record Centre (NMRC) at Swindon produced aerial photographs. During my visit there Katy Whitaker made me aware of material relating to Sir Alan Cobham and his Flying Circus. Ian Hancock and Huby Fairhead of the Norfolk and Suffolk Aviation Museum at Flixton gave me permission to use information available in the museum, as did artist John Constable Reeve.

Thanks are due to the Librarian of the Royal Aeronautical Society Brian L. Riddle and Assistant Librarian Christine Woodward. Jon Buss, Editor of the *Lynn News*, gave me permission to use some photographs and material of the late Raymond Wilson originally published in the *Lynn News* and *Citizen* newspapers. The Nevil Shute Norway Foundation have been generous in the information they have provided, in particular John Anderson, Vice-President of the Foundation and David Dawson-Taylor, UK Librarian and Webmaster of the Foundation.

Details about the life of Lawrence Edwards were provided by the New Zealand Defence Force Archives, the Alexander Turnbull Library (National Library of New Zealand) and the Christchurch City Libraries in New Zealand. Charles Rollings supplied information about Lawrence Edwards as a prisoner of war, and gave me permission to reproduce the photographs and quotations from his books (see Bibliography). Shropshire County Council Archive Centre in Shrewsbury sent details about C. H. Collet and the Darley brothers. Additional information about C. H. Collet was provided by Southampton City Libraries, in particular Librarian David Hollingworth. Simon McKeon and Vicky Green of the Bexley Local Studies and Archive Centre supplied information about Thomas Keppel North and the Vickers Works in Crayford.

John Coady, Dick Garwood, David Lloyd-Jones and Anthony Maynard were helpful sources on Cobham's Flying Circus. Andrew Dawrant supplied copies of Royal Aero Club Certificates at the RAF Museum in Hendon. Professor John Charmley of the University of East Anglia clarified for me the political cartoon on page 87. Henry Labouchere is a fascinating raconteur on his life in aviation. Calista M. Lucy, Keeper of the Archives at Dulwich College, sent details about the Darley brothers and C. H. Collet. Ben Mullarkey gave me permission to reproduce his painting of the Zeppelin bombing of Snettisham as did Hugh Mullarkey, who originally commissioned the painting. Tom North, of Rougham Hall, Norfolk, was a helpful source about his uncle, the late Thomas Keppel North OBE. Brian Hillman first pointed out to me Thomas North's grave in Rougham Churchyard. Stan Langley provided information and photographs about the Bigg-Wither crash of 1926. Andrew L. Payn, Operations Director of Framlingham College in Suffolk, invited us to inspect Group Captain Pickard's memorabilia at the College and Chris Essex gave me permission to use some of the material and images from the Old Framlinghamian website. Mary Pishorn of Heacham supplied information about the visits of Pauline Gower and Sir Alan Cobham to the local area. Winston G. Ramsey, Editor-in-Chief of *After the Battle*, gave me permission to use some images of Group Captain Pickard. Dr R. V. Smith of BAE Systems has been a useful source of advice. Julian Usborne drew my attention to some of the Norfolk balloon hoaxers and David Paton-Williams supplied information about Katterfelto, one of the best known of them. Mrs Eileen Wilson, widow of the late Raymond Wilson who was Librarian in King's Lynn and a noted local historian and author, passed to me some of her late husband's books and memorabilia with permission to use whatever material I required. Wing Commander Ken Wallis invited me to his home and entertained me with stories about his life in aviation. Robin Whitmore supplied information on General John Money and early ballooning.

I am grateful to NewPrint and Design Ltd of Fakenham, in particular Alastair Robinson and John Newstead. Crown Copyright material is reproduced by permission of the Controller of Her Majesty's Stationery Office. Steve Snelling, former *Eastern Daily Press* Sunday editor, kindly agreed to write the Foreword of this book.

This being the 10th anniversary of the East Anglian Air Ambulance, I hope to donate a percentage of the profits from this book to the charity. I am grateful to the staff of the EAAA for their advice and help, in particular PR Consultant Rebecca George and Area Fundraising Coordinator Ellie Walker.

A special thanks to my sister Elspeth Mackinlay who took on the laborious task of proofreading which saved me from many errors, and to my wife Janet who always maintains that when there is no sign of me around the house (especially when there is gardening or DIY to be done) I can only be in one place – the study.

Peter B. Gunn,
Docking, Norfolk, September 2010.

GLOSSARY

2/Lt	Second Lieutenant
AC	Aircraftman
AFC	Air Force Cross
ACM	Air Chief Marshal
AOC	Air Officer Commanding
ATA	Air Transport Auxiliary
AVM	Air Vice-Marshal
BG	Bomb (Bombardment) Group (USAAF)
BS	Bomb (Bombardment) Squadron (USAAF)
C-in-C	Commander-in-Chief
CO	Commanding Officer
CWGC	Commonwealth War Graves Commission
DFC	Distinguished Flying Cross (there was also an American DFC).
DFC*	Distinguished Flying Cross (asterisk signifies Bar to decoration)
DSC	Distinguished Service Cross (Royal Navy decoration).
DSC	(American) Distinguished Service Cross (2nd highest US decoration).
DSO	Distinguished Service Order
Fg Off.	Flying Officer
Flt Lt	Flight Lieutenant
hp	horse power
Gp Capt.	Group Captain
GR	General Reconnaissance

Lt	Lieutenant
mph	miles per hour
NATO	North Atlantic Treaty Organisation
POW	prisoner of war
PPL	Private Pilot's Licence
RAAF	Royal Australian Air Force
RCAF	Royal Canadian Air Force
RFC	Royal Flying Corps
RNAS	Royal Naval Air Service
RNZAF	Royal New Zealand Air Force
SAAF	South African Air Force
Sqn Ldr	Squadron Leader
USAAF	United States Army Air Force
Wg Cdr	Wing Commander
WRAF	Women's Royal Air Force
WW1	World War One
WW2	World War Two

A note on illustrations:
Picture credits to the late R. Wilson are abbreviated to RW.
Strenuous efforts have been made to trace the owners of copyright material where known but if there are any errors or omissions the author should be contacted.

A Note on Money and Buying Power

Money values in different historical periods mean little unless *buying power* at the time is taken into account.

Prior to decimalisation in 1971 there were twelve pence (d) in a shilling (s) and twenty shillings in a pound. A guinea was one pound, one shilling. Half a crown was two shillings and sixpence – sometimes expressed as 2/6d. Pound(s) in weight are abbreviated to *lb(s)* and ounce(s) to *oz*.

Unlike recent times which have seen almost continuous inflation, prices in the period before 1940 tended to fluctuate and would often rise steeply (usually during wartime) but would then tend to decline often as sharply. There was a sharp rise in prices at the start of the Napoleonic wars in the 1790s, with a fall due to slump after 1815. This was also true of World War One, when there were rising prices up to about 1921 and then a sharp downward movement in the depression which followed. The Wall Street Crash of 1929 led to another severe fall in prices which only slowly began to recover in the years up to 1939. Another point to note is that there were considerable regional variations in an age when transport networks were not as advanced as they are now, particularly in the early nineteenth century.

In 1815 the charge of five shillings for spectators of the balloon ascent in Norwich can be better set in its context if one considers that in 1800 a farm worker was paid around 10s a week but this declined to about 7s 6d in 1817. The best wage that a labourer could expect to earn would be 15s for a six-day week. A weaver in the 1790s could earn up to a maximum of 30s a week although this began to decline steeply as a result of mechanisation. Of the skilled trades, the so-called aristocrats of labour, a London compositor could earn 24s a week in 1790 and a chair-carver as much as £4 per week. The pint of beer could vary from 1½d to 2d (Oh glory days!). The standard loaf (the quartern – 4 lb 5¼ oz.) varied from about 7d to 17d during times of scarcity. It cost up to £2 a year to rent a cottage in 1790 rising to nearly £10 by 1824. Bacon cost around 5d to 8d per lb. At Chelsea Hospital a private's coat in 1815 cost around £1 7s and a pair of shoes 7s.

In the early 1920s, Nevil Shute was paying £5 10s per hour for flying lessons – no wonder he required parental support! The comparable hourly cost of a flying lesson in the Norwich School of Flying in August 2009 was £140.

The five shilling flights offered in Cobham's Flying Circus that schoolboys eagerly saved for in the early 1930s was equivalent to roughly half the weekly council rent for a three-roomed house in Sheffield. The cost of a flight offered by Classic Wings over Norwich in a vintage eight-seater Dragon Rapide in May 2010 was £79 per person.

During the 1920s and 1930s the farm labourer could earn between £1 5s and £1 10s per week – or between £82 and £89 a year, significant in Norfolk as agriculture was such a large sector of the economy at the time. Most working men in the mid-1930s earned between £3 and £4 a week. The minimum weekly wage payable to farm workers in 2009 was around £300 while a skilled worker in the building trades could expect to earn £400+ weekly.

Of the highest paid professionals in the early 1920s a barrister could earn £1,120 a year and a doctor (GP) £750, an engineer £468 and an army officer £390. In 1924 the Austin Seven, the 'Baby Car' sold for £165 but by 1931 this had fallen to about £100.

In Norwich in the early 1920s men's spring overcoats were being advertised from four guineas and a good, cheap lunch at Arnolds Ltd in Yarmouth was available at half a crown. A day excursion by train to Brighton for the Norwich City Supporters Club was advertised at 14s 6d, and to slake the thirst a pint of mild beer would cost 5d or 6d – the impact of duty on alcohol since the war had doubled its price! That British institution the fish-and-chip supper in the 1930s was priced at 3d for cod and 1d for chips.

In the later 1920s the average semi-detached house in Greater London was priced around £600 - £850, and about £500 in the provinces. In the early 1950s a similar house outside London would average between £1,650 and £1,950.

Sources:
Eastern Daily Press, various editions of the early 1920s (Norwich Millennium Library, Local Heritage Centre).
Holmes, Richard, *Redcoat: The British Soldier in the Age of Horse and Musket* (HarperCollins*Publishers* 2001)
Burnett, John, *A Social History of Housing 1815-1985* (Methuen 1980).
"   "   "   *A History of the Cost of Living* (Penguin Books Limited 1969).

1

Balloon Mania and the Norfolk Connection

The birth of modern science and the French pioneers

Orville and Wilbur Wright have always rightly been credited with achieving the world's first manned powered flight on 17 December 1903, and on 16 October 1908 American-born Samuel Franklin Cody made the first officially recognised aeroplane flight in Great Britain piloting British Army Aeroplane No. 1 at Farnborough. It is often forgotten that the first successful manned flights predated that of the Wright brothers by well over 120 years, and that Norfolk was in the forefront of these epic events.

The dream of man to fly through the air must be one of the oldest dreams in existence. The Greek myth of 1700 BC tells of Daedalus and his son Icarus attempting to fly from the clutches of the tyrant King Minos of Greece with the aid of wax and feathers. The experiment proved a disaster for Icarus, whose wings melted in the sun, but Daedalus managed to land safely in Naples. In the centuries that followed little practical progress was made and dreams of flying seemed to be confined to plans and drawings such as those of Leonardo da Vinci (1452-1519). In the course of the eighteenth century the dead hand of religious orthodoxy was beginning to make way for a new spirit of scientific and technological enquiry throughout Europe which in turn opened the way for fresh experimentation. The Age of Faith was being overtaken by the Age of Reason.

By the second half of the eighteenth century investigations were being conducted into the nature of the atmosphere and questions were being asked like 'Why do sparks in a fire rise?' and 'Why does smoke rise?' At its very simplest this suggested that there must be substances or gases which were lighter than air in weight.

A major development was the discovery of hydrogen by Henry Cavendish in 1766, which he called 'Phlogiston' or 'inflammable air' (the gas was only named hydrogen in 1790). Cavendish was an amateur scientist and a member of the Royal Society as well as being a friend of Sir Joseph Banks (President of the Royal Society from 1778). Then in 1774 Joseph Priestley, described as 'the father of modern chemistry', was inspired by the work of Cavendish to undertake studies which he outlined in his book

Experiments and Observations on Different Kinds of Air. He discovered oxygen and pioneered a method of obtaining hydrogen. Priestley's book was translated into French in 1776 and it is said that this encouraged the brothers Joseph and Etienne Montgolfier of Paris to experiment with hot air balloons. In an uncanny similarity with the early Russian space shots of the late 1950s their first major success was in launching a balloon with live animals, a sheep, a cock and a duck, from Versailles on 19 September 1783. The apparatus covered just under two miles in eight minutes, rising to about 1,500 feet, and the animals were none the worse from their experience.

The first flight with aeronauts took place a few weeks later on 21 November in a Montgolfier balloon by Jean-François Pilâtre de Rozier (1754-85), a Professor of Natural Philosophy, and François Laurent, the Marquis d'Arlandes (a Major in the Garde Royale), from the Château La Muette in the Bois de Boulogne, Paris. The paper-lined linen balloon (the Montgolfier family business was paper manufacturing) was heated by a brazier burning straw and travelled just over five and a half miles for 25 minutes at an altitude of about 300 feet. All went well except for a fire which broke out in the brazier below the neck of the balloon but was extinguished by the aeronauts with sponge and water, thus highlighting the dangers of an open fire in a hot-air balloon.

However ambitious this early feat was, there were severe limitations to the usefulness of hot air balloons, and the use of hydrogen or 'Phlogiston' – 'inflammable air' as a lighter-than-air gas, appeared to make possible the lifting of objects into the air by means of the 'negative weight' of the gas, and this opened the way for further balloon experiments. The first recorded manned flight in a hydrogen-filled balloon was made on 1 December 1783 from the Tuileries in Paris by physicist Professor Jacques Charles and Aîné Robert, a mechanic, over a distance of 27 miles rising to about 9,000 feet in a flight lasting for two hours.

Another early balloonist was Jean-Pierre Blanchard who made his first ascent in March 1784 in a Montgolfier balloon from the Champ de Mars in Paris. After a number of other ascents he became disillusioned with his lack of public recognition in France compared to the Montgolfier brothers and Pilâtre de Rozier, and decided to come to England in August 1784. Here he became the centre of an informal 'club' of ballooning enthusiasts which included Lord Foley, the beautiful Duchess of Devonshire Georgiana Cavendish (née Spencer), a Major Gardner, the anatomist Dr

John Sheldon and scientist and doctor of medicine Dr John Jeffries. Jeffries was an American, born in Boston in 1744 who had trained and practised in England for ten years before returning home in 1789. He was a man of great wealth and had been associated with the famous surgeon John Hunter. Georgiana, the Duchess of Devonshire, was at the centre of London social and political life of its day and in more recent times was the subject of the film *The Duchess*, released in 2008, some of whose locations included Holkham Hall and other Norfolk beauty spots.

Balloon mania in Britain

Three men with strong Norfolk associations were also members of this circle, George Walpole, the third Earl of Orford, who although described as a 'rake' and 'eccentric' held the positions of Lord Lieutenant of Norfolk and Colonel of the Norfolk Militia, and Major John Money of Trowse Newton, Norwich (of whom more will be said later). The third Earl of Orford's uncle Horace Walpole was also closely involved as a literary figure and commentator rather than as a practising balloonist. He was the fourth son of Sir Robert Walpole, Britain's first Prime Minister, and had served as Member of Parliament for Castle Rising from 1754-57 and for Lynn from 1757-67. For many years he divided his time between the family seat at Houghton Hall and 'Strawberry Hill' in Twickenham, where he wined and dined many of the ballooning fraternity, including Blanchard and Pilâtre de Rozier.

In 1791 on the death of the third Earl, Horace Walpole succeeded to the title as the fourth Earl of Orford in an unusual arrangement by which he succeeded his own nephew, his elder brother's son. Horace died in 1797 and as he lacked an heir the title went into abeyance until its revival in 1806 in the person of Horatio, the second Lord Walpole of Wolterton, who became the first Earl of Orford of new creation. He died in 1809.

News of the developments in France travelled fast, and on 25 August 1784 the first manned balloon ascent in Great Britain was made by James Tytler from Edinburgh in a Montgolfier-type hot-air balloon. In September Vincent Lunardi, Neapolitan Ambassador in London, made the first manned balloon ascent in England from the Artillery Ground at Moorfields in London. The following month James Sadler of Oxford became the first Englishman to ascend in a balloon, also a Montgolfier-type or 'fire-balloon' as it was then termed, rising to about 3,600 feet in a flight lasting for half an hour over a distance of six miles.

Katterfelto, the 'Prince of Puff' and the Hoaxers

In an age when the dividing line between science, magic, witchcraft and superstition could often be blurred, there was ample opportunity for tricksters and hoaxers to jump on the bandwagon of balloon mania. One such was a gentleman called Gustavus Katterfelto, a German immigrant who had arrived in Hull with his family in 1776 at the age of 33 to set himself up as a roving lecturer and travelling magician. He claimed to possess, amongst other qualifications, a doctorate in science, a professorship in philosophy and a Fellowship of the Royal Society in London, none of which had any basis in fact. Beginning in York he began to travel around the country and when he heard the news about ballooning from France he began to think about adding that expertise to his repertoire. He made it known that he was a pioneer of ballooning, claiming to have launched an air balloon in St Petersburg as far back as 1768 in honour of the Empress of Russia's birthday, a tall story but one which attracted some attention from the public.

In the winter of 1784 Katterfelto arrived in Norwich, equipped with a balloon, and announced he would ascend in a large Air Balloon [sic] with two little black boys to make observations in the upper atmosphere, but on two separate occasions the flight was called off. The following June 1785 he made his way to the Duke's Head in King's Lynn, making sure that the Norwich newspapers were reporting an ascent by 'the Great Philosopher' in a Night Air Balloon [sic] the previous May in front of the King, Queen and Royal Family before Buckingham House and Garden. The London newspapers said nothing about this supposed ascent and nothing came of promised ascents during the rest of 1785 when Katterfelto moved on to stay at the Rose and Crown, Wisbech, and then on to Northampton.

He continued his travels around the country making all sorts of claims which no doubt had at least some entertainment value, until he died penniless in Bedale, Yorkshire, in 1799 and was buried in a tomb below the altar rails of the church.

The 'Aerostatick Stage Balloon'. One of many satires on balloon ascents c. 1783. At the top sit three society ladies known for their 'amours' at the time. In the centre (middle) sit politicians (ex-ministers) Lord North, his arm on Charles James Fox's shoulder. Edmund Burke, statesman and political philosopher, sits to the right looking at the Pope, and on the left the Devil looks on. On the lowest gallery sit a group of celebrated 'quacks', and on the right sits Katterfelto gazing at the moon, his black cat facing him asking 'are there any Mice in the Moon, Master?'

"And Katerfelto, with his hair on end
At his own wonders, wondering for his bread."

William Cowper

*Katterfelto in ghostly pose pointing to his own tomb in St Gregory's Church, Bedale, North Yorkshire (*alias *the Revd David Paton-Williams, Rector 1998-2008)*

James Deeker

Reality asserted itself on 7 January 1785 when Blanchard and Dr John Jeffries made the first manned balloon crossing of the English Channel. The enterprise was assisted by James Deeker, a hitherto obscure seller of experimental balloons at a shop in Berwick Street, Soho. The balloon was launched from Dover Castle and ended with a landing in the forest of Guînes, near Ardres, northern France.

It was James Deeker who made the first known manned flight in a balloon in Norfolk on 1 June 1785, from Quantrell's Gardens in Norwich. Deeker prepared the 'Royal Balloon' and got ready to ascend with a 14-year old girl named Miss Weller. The moment of launch coincided with a thunderstorm and some of the balloon's fabric was damaged and gas escaped. After the storm had passed Deeker set off but was forced to leave Miss Weller behind. According to a contemporary account the balloon rose and 'when ascended but a little way he [Deeker] looked downwards, and was much struck with the appearance of the city of Norwich. It seemed to be a large and level collection of buildings, having a great number of intermediate spaces compleatly [sic] filled with faces, all which seemed remarkably white and turned in a direction toward him. He could clearly distinguish the brow of Mousehold Heath, the Castlehill, the tops of churches, many scaffolds, Quantrell's Gardens, the adjoining roads and fields, in like manner covered with faces, and he for some time heard many acclamations.' Deeker travelled eastwards but could only reach Sizeland near Loddon, about ten miles from Norwich. He made a second flight on 23 June, this time in a high wind, and as the balloon was not fully inflated Miss Weller was once again left behind. This time he travelled to Topcroft, twelve miles from Norwich, 'some horsemen who had followed him helping to secure the balloon'.

John Money

It was at this time that a remarkable Norfolk character named Major John Money stepped into the picture. Born in 1739/1740 (the apparent discrepancy due to the adoption of the Gregorian Calendar to replace the Julian Calendar in 1752 which meant that the date was advanced by 11 days), he was the son of a tenant farmer at Trowse Newton named William Money. When old enough John joined the Norfolk Militia and then served as a cornet in the 6th Enniskillen Dragoons. During the Seven Years' War (1756-63) he became a volunteer in Elliot's Light Horse, and was present at the battle of Tillinghausen. By 1771 he had transferred to the 9th (Norfolk) Regiment of Foot as a captain and served with his regiment in the American Revolutionary War (1775-1782) in which he held the position of Deputy-Assistant Quarter-Master-General of the army commanded by General Burgoyne. Burgoyne's army was surrounded by Washington's forces at Saratoga and surrendered on 16 October 1777 – a black day in the history of the British army – and some 3,000 men, including Money, became prisoners of war for the next three years.

On his return to England in 1781 Money continued to serve in the army but retired from the service as a major on half pay in 1784. On his estate at Trowse Newton he built a mansion called Crown Point (named after a place he was said to have known in North America), better known today as Whitlingham Hall, built on the site of Money's mansion. This was close to the location of his father's farm, which had been attacked and ransacked by the mob during the food riots of 1766.

If anyone had imagined that John Money in his mid-forties would now settle for the sedate lifestyle of a prosperous country squire, content with overseeing his 3-400 acre estate and enjoying the social life of the Norfolk landed gentry, they would have been greatly mistaken. Hungry for further challenge, he developed a new interest in ballooning, without doubt kindled by his military experience in the need for accurate observation of enemy dispositions and movements in battle. Well aware of the growing social circle of enthusiasts on both sides of the Channel, Money eagerly took up the opportunity for himself.

Major John Money's first flight took place only two days after Deeker had ascended from Norwich, on 3 June 1785, from Tottenham Court Road in London, in a balloon with companions Jonathan Lockwood (the balloon owner) and a certain Lieutenant George Blake RN. Tottenham Court Road had been the scene of an earlier successful balloon flight in March of the same year by Count Francesco Zambeccari (1752-1812), an Italian sailor of fortune who had sought refuge in England from the Inquisition. On 3 June, the 'British Balloon', as it was called, was inflated to three quarters of its capacity, an operation assisted by George Biggin and Pilâtre de Rozier. Biggin was another member of the 'balloon set', an Etonian, patron of the arts and amateur chemist – perhaps his most notable achievement being the invention of the coffee percolator! The balloon rose but descended due to a loss of gas and came down near Abridge in Essex. After drawing lots it was decided that Blake should vacate the balloon, and it rose again with Money and Lockwood before finally descending about eight miles from Maldon in Essex, a total distance covered of 40 miles. Later Money and Blake dined with Lord Orford at High Beech in Epping, in the company of Vincent Lunardi's patron George Biggin and Pilâtre de Rozier.

Only days later, on 15 June 1785, Pilâtre de Rozier and Jules Romain were killed at Boulogne while attempting to cross the Channel in a combined Montgolfier-type and 'Charlière' (hydrogen) balloon. Thus the world's first aeronaut perished in the world's first aerial disaster.

Not in any way discouraged by these events, on 23 July 1785 Major Money ascended in a balloon, advertised in the *Norwich Mercury* as 'The British Balloon' and 'the finest balloon in England', from Quantrell's Gardens in Norwich before a crowd of several thousand spectators. This was in fact Count Zambeccari's balloon, a contraption said to be 'the only one that is capable of ascending with three persons; and as the expence [sic] attending the filling is so great, it is probable that no such balloon will ever be seen again in this county'. The plan had been for Blake and Lockwood to accompany Money once again, but due to inadequate inflation the balloon could only carry one person. It was intended that the proceeds from the event would go to the Norfolk and Norwich Hospital. Unfortunately the gas-release valve was faulty and it refused to open, and Major Money was unable to make a landfall, instead drifting out to sea for over two hours until he came down 20 miles off Southwold at around six o' clock in the evening. Various boats from Lowestoft and Southwold were unable to locate him in the growing darkness and fears grew for his safety. Money struggled to stay afloat (the fact that the gas release valve could not open must have helped save him) and a Dutch boat saw him clinging to the balloon but did not stop, fearing that the balloon was some kind of sea monster. He remained in the water for five hours until at 11.30 pm he was rescued by the Harwich-based revenue cutter *Argus*, captained by William Haggas, taken to Lowestoft none the worse for the ordeal and fortified by a few glasses of grog (which he pronounced far more delicious than champagne). Apparently the town of Lowestoft were in raptures about the adventure and Money became a local celebrity, before taking a post-chaise back to his home at Crown Point. This was the first rescue from the sea of an aeronaut.

'The Perilous Situation of Major Money', 23 July 1785. (Norfolk Local Studies Library).

The entire episode became the subject of an epic poem written a few years later by Money's friend and fellow soldier, the First Marquis Townshend (1724-1807), entitled *A Poetical Epistle on Major Money's Ascent in a Balloon from the City of Norwich and his Descent into the Sea*. While expressing admiration for Money's courage, Marquis Townshend gently chided him for what seemed like a reckless adventure.

The old adage that you can never believe anything you read in newspapers can never have been more true than in October 1785 when the London newspapers described in detail a balloon flight from Beccles in Suffolk by the Reverend Peter Routh, headmaster of the local grammar school, in company with a Mr Robert Davy and a Miss Hines. In an uncanny resemblance to Major Money's escapade it was reported that Routh's balloon was observed near Yarmouth and blown out to sea until it landed off the coast of Holland where a Dutch boat rescued the occupants and brought them back safely to Beccles. A marble memorial and inscription was planned for the church as a thank-offering for divine deliverance. A few days later on 22 October the *Norwich Mercury* reported that the story was a complete hoax, merely an attempt 'to ridicule a worthy and respectable character'. There was never a memorial in the church. Peter Routh was an elderly curate and classical scholar and the last person who would have attempted a balloon flight. The hoaxer was never identified and his motives were unknown. Perhaps there was a hidden grudge against schoolmasters.

Another very plausible account of a flight which never took place was related in the *London Chronicle* of 22 July 1786 from Coltishall near Norwich by a William Perkins Esq., a gentleman of 'great philosophical experience' with his daughter. The flight, in a balloon 30 feet in diameter supposedly took place from eleven o' clock until safely landing at about two o'clock. Once again there was no clue as to the origin of the spoof.[1]

Money's military adventures were far from over, although he often seemed to have the knack of finding himself on the losing side. He participated for a time on the side of the Belgians in the rebellion against Austrian rule, in which he was granted a commission as major-general, and after 1789 was present in Paris during the French Revolution in the service of the French King Louis XVI, but left shortly before the king was executed. He maintained his interest in the military possibilities of ballooning as outlined in *A Short Treatise on the use of Balloons and Field Observators in Military Operations*, issued in 1803. He continued to develop his ideas in military theory, on the need for light, mobile infantry and on army reform, constantly badgering the government on the subject of coastal defence against the threat of French invasion. In 1806 he addressed a letter to William Windham, Secretary of State for War and the Colonies, a Whig politician and former MP for Norwich (but now Member for a Cornwall seat) and a fellow ballooning enthusiast, on the defence of London against a French invasion. Windham was a member of the distinguished family that owned Felbrigg Hall (where he was buried after his death in 1809).

Sadler and sons

With the onset of the French wars, ballooning mania seemed to cool, as more serious issues asserted themselves and it was after a gap of several years that James Sadler resumed ballooning from about 1810. On 7 October 1811 he was accompanied by a man named John Burcham of East Dereham on a flight from Vauxhall, near Birmingham, over a distance of 112 miles in 80 minutes. Drifting towards Market Deeping the towns of Peterborough, Stamford, Wisbech and Crowland came into view until they 'struck the earth' and Sadler was 'thrown violently out'. The balloon continued with Burcham for another one and a half miles until the envelope was caught in a tree and ripped to shreds 'and Mr Burcham was fortunately relieved from his perilous situation and safely landed on *terra firma* with only a slight bruize' [sic]. The two aeronauts met up later, with great relief, in Heckington near Spalding in Lincolnshire.

Sadler nearly came to a much worse fate during October of the following year, when he came down while attempting to cross the Irish Sea from Dublin to Holyhead. Fortunately, like John Money, he was picked up in time by a herring boat and was landed safely at Liverpool.

A curious incident took place in early 1815, when a Mr Steward advertised in the *Norwich Mercury* of Saturday 4 February a balloon ascent from Prussia Gardens, Norwich, with tickets for spectators being available for 'five shillings or five for a guinea'. Thursday 9 February was the great day for the 'Ascension' [sic]. Some 50,000 people were watching as the balloon left the ground but travelled about 150 feet only to fall in 'Mr Hall's garden, never to rise again'. The crowd felt they had been cheated and in their anger ripped the balloon to pieces and Steward just managed to escape in the carriage of General Money, who happened to be in the right place at the right time.

On Saturday 15 July 1815, barely a month after the Battle of Waterloo, the *Norwich Mercury* announced that Mr Sadler, late member of the Board of Naval Works, would make his 46th ascent in a balloon on 29 July from Ranelagh Gardens, Norwich. This was a reference to James Sadler, the pioneer balloonist, although he was by this time in his sixties, and many of the ascents were by now being made by his son William Windham Sadler. Windham had accompanied James Sadler in May 1785 in a balloon from Moulsey Hurst. It seems to be more than a coincidence that this was the middle name of one of James Sadler's sons. There was in addition John, James Sadler's eldest son, also a balloonist. Occasionally William Sadler was billed as 'Mr Sadler, jnr'. Once again the tickets were available at what seemed to be the going rate for such an event of five shillings each or five for a guinea. It must have been quite an occasion for the several thousand people reported to have gathered, on a fine warm day with not a cloud in the sky and with a musical band in attendance. General Money was also present, some 30 years after his own rescue out to sea. The firing of a gun signalled the start of the event and Mr Sadler's balloon rose into the air, travelling for three miles until landfall in a field near Sprowston Hall an hour and a quarter later. A few weeks later on 1 September James Sadler made his 47th ascent at Newcastle-upon-Tyne. His son Windham Sadler continued his ballooning exploits until his death in an accident during his 31st ascent at Blackburn in September 1824. James Sadler, the pioneer aeronaut, outlived his sons and died at Oxford in 1828.

Later developments

General Money maintained his interest in ballooning right up to his last days. His grave is at St Andrew's Church, Trowse, and on his tomb adjacent to the church is the simple inscription 'General John Money, Died March 26 1817, Aged 77 Years'. He was a significant pioneer of early aviation and the first soldier to become airborne. He produced the first systematic study of the potential of balloons in military operations, although there is little evidence that his influence carried any weight with the government of the day. Apart from anything else he was a remarkable and versatile character, a soldier, adventurer, military theorist and a considerable figure in the Norfolk society of its day, remembered especially for the annual ball he hosted at Crown Point.

Some years later, on a Wednesday in September 1825, there was a balloon flight from Richmond Hill Gardens, Norwich (in the area of the present-day Southgate Lane), organised by a Mr Graham in the company of Colonel John Harvey of Thorpe Lodge, High Sheriff of Norfolk. The apparatus failed to get into the air due to excess weight, so Colonel Harvey took off his hat and coat and Mrs Graham changed places with her husband and the balloon successfully ascended – it would be interesting to speculate on the difference in size and shape of husband and wife. A distance of six and a half miles was covered in 19 minutes, and it appears that Mrs Graham was the first lady to fly in Norfolk!

Charles Green

Pioneer balloonist Charles Green was the first to substitute coal gas for hydrogen, a much cheaper and less volatile gas for its purpose. His first ascent had been from the Green Park in London in July 1821 as part of the celebrations for the Coronation of King George IV. On 21 June 1826 he made a successful ascent from Lynn Gas Works, South Lynn, in the presence of some 15,000 spectators for which adults were charged 2/6d (half-a-crown), and children were admitted for half price. The balloon landed safely at Southery near Downham Market. Green was to make a return visit to King's Lynn in 1827.

In September 1835 he undertook a voyage from Vauxhall Gardens in London in the company of a surgeon named Butler. They landed at Walthamstow and Butler got out. Green took off again and remained in the air all night, eventually landing at Downham Market in Norfolk. He breakfasted and then reascended, finally landing at Lynn in a flight lasting for a total of 13 hours over a distance of at least 130 miles.

In later years Green's achievements included a long distance record in ballooning from London to Nassau in Germany in 1836, and a height record of 27,146 feet in 1837. Towards the end of his ballooning career he made a number of flights from towns in the southern counties, including one from Norwich on 4 September 1849. On this occasion he was accompanied by George Rush of Elsenham Hall in Essex, a wealthy gentleman who was experimenting with an 'improved' aneroid barometer as a means of indicating height. This was Rush's 13th ascent and his aim was to test the density of the atmosphere at varying heights. The 'Victoria' balloon ascended from the Cavalry Barracks in Norwich, passing over the East Anglian Railway between Dereham and Swaffham, continuing towards the Wash and passing the ruins of Appleton Church before descending after about two hours in a field at West Newton[2].

Most of Green's remaining balloon ascents were from Vauxhall Gardens until he made a final flight in 1852. In his lifetime he made 526 balloon ascents. In later years he lived in Highgate and attended the early meetings of the newly formed Aeronautical Society (founded in 1866). He died in March 1870 at the age of eighty-five.

The legacy

Progress in ballooning was very much more in evidence in other countries, notably the United States and France. A military use in aerial reconnaissance was demonstrated in the American Civil War when the U.S. Army Balloon Corps was formed in October 1861 with five balloons and 50 men.

Proven experience in ballooning and interest in aeronautics in general led to the formation of the Aeronautical Society of Great Britain in January 1866. By this time interest was growing in the possibilities of heavier-than-air machines.

The military potential of aviation was for the first time acknowledged by the War Office in 1878 when £150 was allocated for balloon development. Captain James Lethbridge Brooke Templer of the 2nd Middlesex Militia, an experienced balloonist, became the first British air commander. The British Army's Balloon School was set up in Chatham, Kent, in 1883 later moving to Aldershot. A man-lifting kite section was established in 1894 but little appears to have come of this. Before long budding aviators were turning their attention to more substantial contraptions although the legacy of these experiments in ballooning was to be the German Zeppelins of the Great War and the R-series of airships in Britain afterwards, which came to a tragic conclusion with the R101 disaster in Beauvais in France in October 1930.

Notes:
[1] I am grateful to Julian Usborne for making me aware of these hoaxes.
[2] *Norfolk Annals*, quoted in EDP 27 September 2008. Also George Rush, *Account of Ascents of Nassau and Victoria Balloons 1838, 1849 and 1850.*

2

Charles Herbert Collet – Pioneer Marine Aviator

First aeroplane over West Norfolk?

On Wednesday 10 May 1914 the people of West Norfolk were treated to the unfamiliar sight and sound of a flying machine, believed to have been one of the first aeroplanes ever to have flown over this part of the eastern counties. The pilot was Lieutenant Charles Herbert Collet of the Royal Marine Artillery, and one of the first members of the fledgling Naval Wing of the Royal Flying Corps. The aircraft was a DFW (short for Deutsche Flugzeugwerke) all-steel Military Arrow Tractor Biplane No. 154, built in Leipzig and acquired by the Admiralty earlier that year, and Collet was attempting a long-distance flight from Gosport in Hampshire to Wick in Caithness. Equipped with a 100 hp Mercedes engine it was an advanced aircraft for its day, capable of a speed range of between 45 and 85 mph and a rate of climb to 3,500 feet in four minutes. For the flight a large petrol tank had been fitted in place of the passenger's seat. Lieutenant Collet had taken off at 7.30 in the morning from Gosport on 10 May with a petrol, oil and water load of 125 gallons on what he hoped would be a record-breaking non-stop flight. Battling with a strong north-easterly wind he fought his way across southern England and East Anglia before engine trouble forced him to make an unscheduled landing near Donna Nook in Lincolnshire after seven and a half hours in the air. In spite of the disappointment, Collet had actually achieved one of the longest flights recorded at that time. He blazed a trail in aviation record-breaking which others would follow.

I first read about Collet's flight in an article by the late Raymond Wilson, a noted local historian, in the King's Lynn *Citizen* (14 November 1990) and I became intrigued about this young airman's pioneering flight and his subsequent career. The record of his flying career was one of skill, daring and distinction until it was brought to a premature end by a tragic accident.

Early life

Charles Collet was born in Calcutta in 1888, the second of three sons of James Herbert Collet, a civil engineer, and Teresa Collet (née Pilling). Within a few years the family had left India and settled in Guernsey, where young Charles and brothers Francis and Ralph attended school at Elizabeth College. By the turn of the century the family had moved to Southampton and the brothers were sent to Dulwich College, a leading English public school whose alumni included P. G. Wodehouse and many contemporaries who were to distinguish themselves as aviators in the Great War like the Darley brothers (see Chapter 3). Other Old Alleynians (as the former pupils of Dulwich College were termed) included a contemporary of P. G. Wodehouse, Captain (later Major) Charles Gilson, a distinguished soldier who became one of the leading contributors to *The Boy's Own Paper* with its stirring tales of daring and adventure centred on Britain and its Empire.

Much of this atmosphere must have rubbed off on Charles Collet, for he set his sights on a naval career and entered the Royal Naval College at Greenwich in 1905. By the summer of 1906 he was commissioned as a Lieutenant in the Royal Marine Artillery and in the years which followed excelled at his chosen sports of shooting and boxing. In 1907 he won the Navy and Marine Light Weight Boxing Championship and in 1912 was in the HMS *Duncan* Shooting Team, winners of the Pembroke Camp Challenge Cup (HMS *Pembroke* was the Royal Naval Barracks at Chatham). Eager for a fresh challenge he applied to join the Naval Wing of the Royal Flying Corps and was posted to the Central Flying School at Upavon in Wiltshire on 17 September 1913. This was no mean achievement as competition was stiff for places among Marine and Naval officers for the flying course. When it was first established in 1911 there were only four places available for over 200 applicants, their enthusiasm in no way diminished by the warning that damage to the machines would have to be paid for and students were required to be unmarried. Nothing daunted, Collet took to the air in an Avro Biplane and qualifed as a pilot in just over a month, being awarded Royal Aero Club Certificate No. 666 on 21 October 1913. He was appointed a Flying Officer at the Isle of Grain air station at the end of December and on 17 January 1914 was posted to Eastchurch, which had been established as the first naval air station in 1911. There he joined a small band of aviators under the command of the legendary Commander Charles R. Samson.

Lieutenant Collet was not long in coming to the attention of his superiors as a skilled airman, being selected to test fly the newly acquired DFW aeroplane at Brooklands, which had become a major centre for the manufacturing and testing of the early aeroplanes.

COLLET, Charles Herbert

_____

Born 4th February 1888, **at** Calcutta

Nationality British

Rank, Regiment, Profession Lieut., R.M.A.

Certificate taken on Avro Biplane

At The Central Flying School, Upavon, Wilts.

Date 21st October 1913

Killed 19/8/15 Imbros island, Greece.

Royal Aero Club Certificate of Charles Collet. (Reproduced by kind permission of the Royal Aero Club via Andrew Dawrant)

Lt Collet of Naval Wing RFC in pilot's seat of DFW at Leipzig prior to his testing the machine at Brooklands. (Flightglobal Archive 29 May 1914 page 572)

DFW Arrow flown by Lt Collet, 1914. (RW from the Citizen 14/11/1990)

Collet flying at Brooklands, 1914. (Flightglobal Archive 25 Sept. 1914 page 972)

Brooklands hosted the first aeroplane trials by A. V. Roe in June 1908 and soon it was attracting pioneers like Tommy Sopwith who learned to fly there in 1910 – later Sopwith was to form the Sopwith and later the Hawker aircraft companies which produced many of the most famous of Britain's fighter aircraft. In 1911 the collection of wooden sheds at Brooklands became known as Brooklands Flying Village which housed many of the great aviation pioneers up to 1914. The 1960s film 'Those Magnificent Men in their Flying Machines' was based on the story of these early aviators.

After his long cross-country flight Collet continued to fly the DFW and other aircraft at Brooklands and was reported to have looped the loop in a Caudron in early June, reputedly the first naval airman ever to have done so. Even the *Times* commented on his skilled handling of the DFW where the machine 'suddenly came to life and was made to perform startling tricks – to see him (Collet) descend for a thousand feet or so in a closely-wound spiral and the machine standing vertically on one wing-tip, was an education in the handling of big aeroplanes.' His reputation had gone before him as *Flight* magazine in July 1914 referred to his 'masterful handling' of the DFW at Brooklands which made him the obvious choice for selection to fly the aircraft, re-engined with a Beardmore 120 hp engine, in the forthcoming *Daily Mail* £5,000 Circuit of Britain Race, scheduled for Monday 10 August.

The outbreak of war on 4 August postponed all plans for the air races and the naval aviators at Brooklands, including Collet, were ordered to RNAS Eastchurch for active service. By now a flight lieutenant he continued to fly the DFW as part of the Eastchurch (Mobile) Squadron. This unit was responsible for defence of the east coast and was allocated to Lincolnshire, first to Skegness on 11 August, then to Killinghome and finally to Immingham by the end of the month. It was reported on 10 August that the DFW (presumably with Collet as the pilot) had landed with engine trouble at Scarborough Race Course and the German make of the aircraft aroused the suspicion of the locals, resulting in the pilot and passenger being detained for questioning at the local army barracks. The local newspaper reported that the pilot was a naval man and was armed with an army service revolver. After local fears had been allayed and necessary repairs carried out the aircraft took off to resume its patrol.

Perhaps the German origin of the machine was too much to tolerate for the DFW was taken out of service by the end of the year 'for identification reasons' to be dismantled and transported back to RNAS Eastchurch.

Hero of the Düsseldorf Air Raid

Charles Collet was among the first naval airmen from Eastchurch to arrive on the continent after the outbreak of war on 27 August as part of the Naval Wing. There was a motley collection of about 10 aeroplanes to begin with, based at Ostend, Dunkirk and Antwerp. Winston Churchill, First Lord of the Admiralty, spelt out the objective of the unit 'to deny the use of territory within a hundred miles of Dunkirk to German Zeppelins, and to attack with airplanes all airships found replenishing there.' Accordingly, in an attempt to bring the war to the enemy a plan was laid for a bombing attack by naval aircraft on the Zeppelin sheds at Düsseldorf and Cologne. Elaborate preparations for the raid included an advance force of 'cyclist carabineers and armoured motor cars' to mark out a path to a forward base as near as possible to the German frontier, given the fact that Antwerp was over 100 miles from Düsseldorf. The attack was scheduled for 23 September

Airship hangar at Düsseldorf which was bombarded by Lt Collet RNAS, Sept. 1914. (Flightglobal Archive 25 Sept. 1914 page 986)

and at dawn five aircraft took off, including Collet in a Sopwith three-seater tractor biplane.

The party was divided into two, one formation to fly to Cologne to attack the sheds there and the others to make for Düsseldorf. At first the day was clear but after the River Meuse the mist descended and the first group reached Cologne only to find the city shrouded in thick fog and they were unable to find the target and had no choice but to turn back. Collet had better luck in the second group although there were misty conditions over Düsseldorf. He glided down from 6,000 feet and at about 400 feet was able to distinguish the Zeppelin shed and dropped three bombs, in the course of which his aircraft was hit by a 'projectile'. In spite of the problems, all the aircraft to returned to base safely. Damage to the Zeppelin shed was later claimed and *Flight* magazine reported that these and other flights caused 'hysterical alarm' among the Germans.

The raid received widespread publicity and Collet was fêted as a hero, the *Times'* leader of 24 September hailing the episode as 'the most brilliant and daring feat of airmanship yet seen in the war'. The news was even an inspiration to leading aviators of the Imperial Russian Service, as described by the Russian 'ace' M. Agathonoff in a despatch to the London *Morning Post* which also reached the *New York Times*. In the article about Russian aviators he described how Collet's example of low level bombing in the face of heavy fire had left his colleagues in awe of such daring, so much so that 'a Russian general on hearing of such exploits as recounted in English newspapers was apt to be a little "testy" when his own aviators refused to attempt such an undertaking.'[1] He was the first Royal Marine to go into action in the Great War and one of the first aviators to carry out a bombing raid against the enemy homeland, an exploit for which he was awarded the Distinguished Service Order. It was felt that these raids would be a sufficient reprisal and possibly a future deterrent against German plans to mount similar raids – a vain hope as it turned out!

Collet was in the thick of the action throughout the autumn of 1914, taking part in the defence of Antwerp. On 27 October engine failure brought down his Blériot Parasol Monoplane close to enemy lines and the aircraft was shelled into a wreck. This was probably the occasion when he and his observer Corporal Brewe found themselves under fire from both sides, the Belgians mistaking them for Germans. Once again in what seemed to be like an occupational hazard he was taken prisoner but after the truth was established returned to Allied lines. In January 1915 his Maurice Farman

Pusher biplane was damaged in an attack on Ostend but he escaped unscathed.

The Dardanelles campaign

A new phase of the war in 1915 was the ill-fated Dardanelles campaign, the attempt by the Allies to take the war to Germany's ally Turkey by forcing a passage through the Dardanelles Straits towards Constantinople and into the Black Sea, thereby offering a lifeline to the beleaguered Russians. Bombardment by naval vessels proved largely ineffective and a landing by British and ANZAC[2] troops became inevitable.

Charles Collet (now a captain and flight-commander) was sent with his squadron early in 1915 to the island of Imbros to cover the initial landings which took place on 25 April. One of the duties of the squadron was to carry out bombardment spotting for the Royal Navy but he was also heavily engaged in dogfights with Turkish aircraft, later commenting that the Turks put up a better fight than the Germans he had met on the Western Front. He put all his expertise to the test in a favourite stunt, according to two

A poignant photo of Flight Commander Collet (on right of picture) in his 'dug-out' in the Dardanelles, probably only days before his death on Imbros on 19 Aug. 1915. (Southampton and District Pictorial, Southampton City Libraries)

(Hampshire Advertiser 4 Sept. 1915,
Southampton City Libraries).

Australians who were witnesses at the time, when he and a certain Frenchman would descend suddenly on a Turkish trench, skim along the trench line at low level, deliver their bombs and make off before the Turks could recover from their shock. It was not surprising that he was twice mentioned in despatches during his Mediterranean service. Among his other talents was his formidable photographic memory which reputedly enabled him to play chess blindfolded!

Collet's luck finally ran out on 19 August when he took off in a Sopwith 807 Type Seaplane at Imbros on a Mediterranean patrol – another account states that he was taking a machine unfamiliar to him to another aerodrome – and reached a height of 150 feet when the engine stopped. At too low an altitude to regain control and facing powerful air currents from adjacent cliffs, the aircraft stalled and crashed to the ground, bursting into flames. A valiant attempt to save the pilot was made by Chief Petty Officer Michael Keogh of HMS *Ark Royal* who happened to be at the scene, but the flames overcame him and Collet perished. Later CPO Keogh was awarded the Albert Medal for his bravery.

Charles Collet was laid to rest in Lancashire Landing Cemetery, one of over 30 Commonwealth War Cemeteries on the peninsula, named in honour of the Lancashire Fusiliers who landed on the beach there. The cemetery contains a total of 1,237 British and Commonwealth graves.

By a strange twist of fate Charles Collet's brother Ralph was also a pilot in the RNAS and was faced with a similar misfortune, according to his father's account, when he took off in an aircraft which he was delivering to another aerodrome, and at low altitude the engine failed and he crashed, but this time without fire erupting. He sustained a permanently injured foot and was lucky to survive subsequent blood poisoning. He was invalided out of the Service having been awarded the Distinguished Service Cross and the Belgian Order of the Crown (Chevalier). Charles' other brother Francis also served in the war, attaining the rank of captain in the Royal Engineers.[3]

Charles Collet's aviation career spanned less than two years but his record in aviation during that time must be almost without equal. He was amongst the first of that pioneering band of naval airmen and one of the earliest test pilots. He undertook one of the longest non-stop flights recorded at the time which would be an example to others in later years. He was among the first naval airmen to go into action on the Western Front in 1914 and the first Royal Marine officer to do so. He is generally recognised to have been the first pilot to have carried out an offensive bombing raid into enemy territory during the Great War. Any one of these achievements would have secured for Charles Herbert Collet an enduring place in the story of British aviation.

Notes:

[1] Extract from letter of J. F. H. Collet (17 November 1921), courtesy of Southampton City Libraries Archives.

[2] Australian and New Zealand Army Corps.

[3] Extract from letter of J. F. H. Collet (29 August 1919), courtesy of Southampton City Libraries Archives.

3

The Darleys – Brothers-in-Arms at War

Charles Curtis Darley and Cecil Hill Darley were pilots with distinguished records in the Great War, but fate was to bring them together at Bircham Newton for a flight to disaster in which one of them was to lose his life.

Cecil Hill Darley

Cecil Hill Darley was born on 11 March 1889, eldest son of Captain Charles Edward Darley, late of the Bengal Marines, and Emily Louisa Darley, at Newport in Shropshire. His parents' address was at that time Caynton Manor in Shropshire but later 77 Fountain Road, Edgbaston, Birmingham. He was educated at Dulwich College and Liverpool University, where he took his B.Eng. and later his A.M.I.C.E. (Associate Member of the Institution of Civil Engineers) of London. Early in 1914 he went to Canada and on the outbreak of war was in Montreal and then decided to train as a pilot. He attended the Curtiss School at Toronto and learned to fly on the Curtiss Biplane, qualifying as a pilot with Royal Aero Club Certificate No. 1718 on 1 September 1915. Arriving in England with the first batch of Canadians, he joined the Royal Naval Air Service.[1]

Cecil Darley's first posting was to No. 7 Squadron, No. 4 Wing RNAS at Eastchurch at the end of 1915. In January 1916 he was slightly injured when his aircraft failed to gain height in turning down wind in gusty weather and hit the ground. The Court of Enquiry blamed Darley's handling of the aircraft but he was still rated 'an exceptional pilot'. By the spring the squadron had moved to Dunkirk where Flight Sub-Lieutenant Darley began to take part in bombing operations. On one occasion, on 21 May, he had another mishap, perhaps a foretaste for the future, when his aircraft hit telegraph wires as he took off for a raid on Mariakerke, but this time he escaped unscathed.

Throughout much of 1916 Cecil Darley was flying a Caudron aircraft and taking part in some daring bombing raids, attacking St Denis Westrem aerodrome on 2 August, Tirpitz battery and Handzaeme aerodrome in September, and the docks and ships around Ostende and Zeebrugge Mole in November. On occasions he was also flying Short bombers, which were available to his squadron. At the end of the year he was promoted to flight lieutenant.

On 16 February 1917 Darley was operating from Petite Synthe on a raid to Ghistelles in which he dropped seven 65lb bombs from a height of 5,700 feet, one bomb remaining hung up but he returned safely. For much of that early spring flying was cancelled due to weather conditions but whenever possible bombing operations were carried out against such targets as St Denis Westrem aerodrome, Ostende seaplane base and Zeebrugge Mole. On 30 April Darley was commended for a successful bombing raid on Zeebrugge which was followed by the award of the Distinguished Service Cross on 11 August 1917 for conspicuous skill and gallantry on the night of the 2nd July 1917 on a raid to Bruges. One of his engines seized whilst he was over the target, but he dropped his bombs on the objective and managed to fly his machine home on one engine to a safe landing.

By this time Darley was an acting flight commander and on 28 July the squadron had reformed from part of No. 7 Squadron and renumbered No. 7A Squadron, re-equipping with the Handley Page 0/100, forerunner of the Handley Page series of heavy bombers. Operations continued throughout the year to targets which included Bruges Docks and Thorout aerodrome and Darley was amassing considerable experience as a seasoned night bomber pilot. At the end of 1917 the squadron was renumbered No. 14 Squadron RNAS.

The start of 1918 saw no let-up in bombing operations. On the night of 18th/19th February, Darley carried out two bombing attacks on St Denis Westrem aerodrome, the longest double trip successfully performed up to that date. Since August of the previous year Darley had carried out 30 more night bombing raids, gaining a Bar to his DSC on 17 April.

With the formation of the Royal Air Force on 1 April 1918 the squadron was renumbered No. 214 Squadron RAF, and Cecil Darley was gazetted a captain in the new service. The tempo of night operations continued unabated and on 28 May 1918 he was chosen to carry out an attack on the lock gates at the northern end of the Bruges-Zeebrugge Canal at low water. Had the plan succeeded all vessels would have been stranded in the system. Darley glided into the target, and at 200 feet and in the face of heavy anti-aircraft fire released three 520lb bombs, two of which fell in the water, while the third detonated close to the northern gate. Neither this attack, nor another a few minutes later by a DH4 (shot down by anti-aircraft fire), was successful, but Darley returned safely to his home aerodrome at dawn. For this and previous exploits he received the Distinguished Flying

Cross, as announced in the London Gazette of 2 July 1918 (Citation 3 August 1918). Having carried out nearly 70 bombing operations, mostly at night, he had become one of the most experienced and skilled bomber pilots on the Western Front. A well-earned leave was due and on 21 August he was given permission to travel to Switzerland in civilian clothes, but his war was by no means over.

In the course of 1917 a new and terrifying feature of war had appeared, the advent of strategic bombing of civilian targets. Admittedly there had been the Zeppelin raids earlier in the war, but these had been only pinpricks compared to the threat posed by the new heavy bombers like the German Gothas which from May 1917 began to carry out a series of raids over England, including London, causing considerable damage and loss of life, far in excess of that experienced in the Zeppelin raids. In order to meet this threat Major-General Hugh Trenchard was given the task of organising the Independent Air Force in the course of June 1918 to strike back at targets behind enemy lines. Trenchard was a great believer in strategic bombing and began to organise attacks on rail and industrial centres in Germany.

Initially the force was based in France, using bombers like the twin-engined Handley Page 0/400, but by the summer of 1918 the much more ambitious scheme was to have the force based in England as No. 27 Group, with two Wings, the 86th Wing to operate from England and the 87th from overseas. After some debate it was decided to establish No. 27 Group at Bircham Newton, which was considered to be the most suitable eastern airfield from which to operate heavy bombers and Lieutenant-Colonel Redford Henry Mulock DSO, a Canadian and veteran fighter ace, was appointed to command the Group. By a strange turn of fate his Intelligence Officer was none other than a Royal Navy officer by the name of Erskine Childers, author of the spy story *Riddle of the Sands* and later executed in 1922 as an Irish Nationalist and member of the IRA and opponent of the treaty with the British.[2]

The objective was to bomb Berlin and the means were to hand in the shape of the Handley Page V/1500 or the 'Super Handley Page', the largest British bomber to date and the first with four engines, which had only made its maiden flight in May 1918. The aircraft had considerable potential, capable of carrying thirty 250lb bombs, with a crew of six and an endurance of 1,300 miles at an average speed of around 80 mph, which in reasonable weather was expected to bring Berlin well into its range. In June 1918 No.

Locations of Cecil Darley's flights, 1919

Not to scale

X - Crash site at Lake Bracciano, Italy.

Bircham Newton

France

Biarritz

Pau St Raphael Italy

Madrid

Spain

Rome

Handley Page V/1500 and personnel at Bircham Newton, 1918.
(RAF Museum photo ref. PO 13331)

166 Squadron was the first squadron to be mobilised for 27 Group, equipped with the new V/1500. Major C. H. Darley was appointed squadron commander as he was reputed to have carried out more night bombing raids than anyone else, and he was joined by other carefully selected pilots and observers, many of them Canadian, seasoned in bombing operations in aircraft like the FE2b and Handley Page 0/100 and 0/400 series.

Darley had a formidable task on his hands as production difficulties slowed the expected delivery of the new machines. He himself had to go to one of the subcontracting firms near Glasgow, Wm Beardmore of Dalmuir, to arrange collection of the aircraft, only three of which were available by the time of the Armistice. In the meantime the crews were sent on a course in navigation at Andover and by September there were about 17 officers and 308 other ranks on squadron strength. By 5 November two aircraft were ready for what even Darley admitted was probably a one-way ticket, given the lack of navigational aids, the vagaries of the weather and the untried nature of the task. Plans had been finalised for a landfall in Czechoslovakia should the need arise. As it turned out the operation was delayed by poor weather and on 11 November the Armistice was signed and the Foreign Office ordered a stand-down 'much to the disquiet of the personnel'.[3] 'So Trenchard's plans for 1919, which included "shuttle raids" from Allied bases in Norfolk, Nancy and Prague against every part of Germany, including Berlin, came to nothing.'[4]

Darley continued in post over the winter of 1918-19 while the 'Super Handley-Pages' with their folded wings 'eventually deteriorated to such an extent in the sheds at Bircham Newton that they were reduced to produce'[5]. No. 166 Squadron was disbanded there at the end of May 1919, but there were fresh challenges ahead for Cecil Darley. His skill and experience made him an ideal choice for organising new peacetime roles for some of the surplus heavy aircraft like the V/1500 and the recently introduced Vickers Vimy. He was charged with the task of flying a V/1500 on a non-stop flight to Madrid to advertise its civilian potential to none other than King Alfonso XIII. He took off from Ramsgate but was unable to cross the Pyrenees owing to mist and low cloud, making landfall instead at Pau in south-west France. On resuming his journey the mountains were crossed safely and he reached Madrid in three-and-a-half hours. While in Madrid he led a formation of the super Handley Page, two DH4s and a Bristol Fighter, carrying Spanish government representatives as passengers. However on the return flight his luck ran out and he faced near disaster as his aircraft crashed in the sea off Biarritz. Luckily Darley and his crew struggled to dry land and survived but the aircraft was a write-off. In no way discouraged, Cecil Darley was soon to find another outlet for his energy and ambition. In the meantime the Spanish Government had recognised his achievements by awarding him the Diploma of Military Merit 2nd class.

Charles Curtis Darley

Charles was born on 31 July 1890 at Tibberton in Shropshire and like his brother Cecil was educated at Dulwich College where he excelled at sport, especially rugby, shooting, boxing, fencing and athletics. After school he took a different direction from Cecil and entered the Royal Military Academy at Woolwich, being commissioned into the Royal Field Artillery in 1910. His first posting was to India where in 1911-12 he won the officers' heavy and middleweight boxing championships. He trained as a pilot at the Bristol School in Brooklands on the Bristol Biplane and achieved Royal Aero Club Certificate No. 592 in August 1913 and the following year was seconded to the Royal Flying Corps. For a time he was based at Netheravon, where he instructed A. J. Insall, the brother of G. S. M. Insall (see Chapter 6). On one occasion he set off with A. J. Insall in a Henri Farman No. 507 to have lunch with an aunt who lived in Bath. Insall had no choice but to sit on the petrol tank behind the pilot for the ride, but unfortunately en route a strut became loose and they had to make an emergency landing in a farmer's field. Unable to find the farmer the aviators had to attempt a 'Heath Robinson' repair themselves, which was successful and the journey continued uneventfully.

At the end of April 1915 Lieutenant C. C. Darley was posted to No. 3 Squadron RFC on the Western Front. On occasions he acted as an observer and as a keen photographer he was in the habit of taking his camera when flying. With his pilot Lieutenant George Pretyman he began to take photographs of the front line from the air, purely as a matter of personal interest. This was fairly unusual at the time and Darley had to obtain his own chemicals for development from Béthune, which was close to the squadron billets. He showed his superiors the results of his work who were at first not very interested as the images were taken no higher than about 4,000 feet in a Blériot and covered only a small area. Later the squadron re-equipped with a few Morane Parasols and the results were more impressive from a higher altitude. Darley then showed his squadron commander John Salmond a set of photographic prints he had taken from a section of the front. Salmond was so impressed that he reported to Trenchard who assigned to Darley the task of photographing from the air an area of the front south of La Bassée where the enemy had been more active than usual. A set of enemy fortifications camouflaged as brickworks were revealed and detailed interpretation provided the information needed for a surprise attack at the weak points of the enemy position. The assault caught the Germans unprepared and demonstrated the potential of aerial photographic reconnaissance. Darley's pioneering work in aerial photography took some time to get recognition but eventually a Wing Photographic section was established under the command of Lieutenant J. T. C. Moore-Brabazon.[6]

In July 1915 Charles Darley joined No. 11 Squadron as flight commander of 'C' Flight in the rank of temporary captain, flying the Vickers FB5 fighter 'Gunbus'. At first the squadron was based at St Omer, shortly moving to Vert Galand, and in September to Villers-Bretonneux. Other squadron members included the brothers A. J. Insall and G. S. M. Insall, the latter being awarded the VC for gallantry later that year.

On 26 October Charles Darley fell victim to the notorious German ace Max Immelmann who with his band of Fokker pilots had established virtual air superiority over the Western Front. He and his observer Lieutenant R. J. Slade were flying over Arras in the direction of Cambrai when they were set upon by Immelmann and in the unequal combat the FB5 was riddled with bullets, spiralled down and crashed. The observer was unhurt but Darley was severely wounded in the arm and thumb, forcing him to land with the use of one arm. At this point it has been claimed that in a gallant gesture Immelmann landed near him and completed the severance of the injured thumb with his pocket-knife, bandaged Darley's hand and saw him off to hospital, albeit as a prisoner![7] The other version of the story is less dramatic but probably nearer the mark, that Slade had to perform the operation but in any case both airmen were captured, and Darley was forced to spend the next two years as a prisoner of war.[8]

Darley's severe wounds to his right arm and the loss of a thumb led to his repatriation via neutral Switzerland on 30 May 1916. Unfit to resume active service he was forced to serve the remainder of the war in a staff appointment, no doubt envious of his brother who had achieved distinction as one of the most experienced bomber pilots on the Western Front and was earmarked for the command of an elite bomber force.

However, Charles Darley eventually returned to active duty as a squadron commander and in May 1919 was appointed officer commanding No. 88 Squadron based in Belgium, flying the Bristol F2B Fighter. In August he resigned his commission in the Royal Field Artillery and was appointed a permanent commission as a captain (flight lieutenant) in the Royal Air Force. Within a few days he had secured a posting to Bircham Newton to join the newly formed No. 274 Squadron, the same station as his brother's No. 166 Squadron. This posting guaranteed a more interesting and varied life than could be had at most RAF stations in peacetime.

The fateful flight

With the ending of the war and the run-down of the Royal Air Force there was a massive surplus of heavy aircraft in stations like Bircham Newton, but if one opportunity had closed down, another was opening up. The Vickers Vimy represented a new generation of heavy bombers with potential for peacetime use, as exemplified by the first non-stop transatlantic crossing by Alcock and Brown in June 1919, just one month after Cecil Darley's near disaster returning from Spain. People began to realise the possibilities of such aircraft over the vast distances and scattered territories of the British Empire. One plan was to create an Indian Postal Service which would involve ferrying large aircraft to the Middle East, and then on to India. Cecil Darley (now in the rank of captain) was given the task of ferrying six surplus Vickers Vimy aircraft to Cairo in September 1919.

This was a daunting task, given the record of similar flights during which almost one third of aircraft setting off had failed to complete the journey due to mechanical failures, the weather conditions and inadequate navigational techniques. At the last minute Cecil Darley's designated navigator Flight Lieutenant Allan Perry-Keene was replaced by Cecil's brother Charles, and with the third crew member AC1 Hollington, the Vimy took off from Bircham Newton on 24 September on its route via St Raphael in southern France where it was delayed by engine trouble. Another crew member, Flight Lieutenant Hudson, joined them for the next leg to Italy and after struggling against severe winds the crew fell short of the intended landfall near Rome and instead reached a landing ground near Lake Bracciano, twenty miles north of Rome.

*Cecil Darley (left foreground) and Charles Darley in front of the Vickers Vimy
about to take off from Bircham Newton for Cairo 24 September 1919.
(Author via Marion M. Newman)*

The Vimy preparing to take off. (RAF Museum photo ref. P008236)

After a night's rest Darley and his crew returned to the aircraft to find that the landing ground was saturated with overnight rain and on a slope which led abruptly to a series of telegraph lines at its foot, making it very marginal for a safe take-off. At nine o' clock on 27 September Darley made the Vimy ready and set off. Desperately trying to pick up speed sufficiently for lift, he wrestled with the controls until it was too late as the Vimy touched one of the posts at the end of the field, the aircraft spun round and crashed to the ground, tipping over in the process before bursting into flames. Charles Darley and Hollington were thrown out but Cecil was trapped in the blazing aeroplane. Seeing his plight, Charles fought his way back to the burning wreck and struggled to free his brother time and time again until flames enveloped him and he eventually collapsed due to severe burns. His brother died in the wreckage.

The grave of Captain Cecil Hill Darley DSC and Bar, DFC, is to be found in the Commonwealth War Graves Commission plot in the Testaccio Protestant Cemetery on the south side of the city of Rome. The *Shrewsbury Chronicle* of 3 October 1919 paid a fulsome tribute to the death of this 'local airman' which would cause deep regret in his home area of Newport, describing Cecil Darley as 'one of the most distinguished and intrepid airmen in the British service'.

Charles Darley survived the ordeal but spent the next eighteen months in hospital as a result of his appalling injuries. Recognition of his heroism was recorded in *The Times* of 19 October 1922 which reported that he was awarded the Albert Medal for bravery by the King, and also 'the Silver Medal and 10 guineas' by the Society for the Protection of Life from Fire.

After recovering from his injuries Charles remained in the Royal Air Force, but due to his injuries was forced to accept a number of staff appointments, which included service in India. In 1936 he was appointed to command No. 10 FTS (Flying Training School) at Ternhill in Shropshire and in 1938 returned to India to command No. 1 (Indian) Group, Peshawar, which was close to the North-West Frontier of Afghanistan. In September 1939 he was invalided out of the Air Force due to a flying accident. He retired as an Air Commodore and was awarded the CBE. He died in June 1962.

Notes:

[1] Wise, S. F., *Canadian Airmen and The First World War* pp 207/208
[2] Jacklin, David, *'The Super Handley'* pp12-17
[3] National Archives, App. 'B' AIR 27, letter of C. C. Darley to Sqn Ldr J. H. C. Wake 1/3/1937.
[4] Boyle, Andrew, *Trenchard* p313.
[5] National Archives, App. 'B' Air 27, op. cit.
[6] Barker, Ralph, *The Royal Flying Corps in France* pp65-6.
[7] Insall, A.J. *Observer: Memoirs of the Royal Flying Corps 1915-18,* pp86-7.
[8] *Shrewsbury Chronicle* 3 October 1919 p4, obit. of C. C. Darley.

4

Thomas Keppel North and the Vickers Vimy

In the unlikely setting of St Mary's Churchyard in the village of Rougham in Norfolk there is a gravestone with an inscription and image which links a quiet and unassuming inventor and engineer with the achievement of the first non-stop transatlantic flight in June 1919. Thomas Keppel North OBE, Superintendent of the Vickers Works at Crayford in Kent, had played a significant role in the design and manufacture of the Vickers Vimy bomber, the type which was to be flown by Alcock and Brown in their epic flight of June 1919. The sad part was that Thomas North never lived to see this triumph, having died of pneumonia only a few months before on 10 February at the age of 42, a victim of the world-wide 'flu pandemic which claimed nearly 30 million lives.

Thomas North was a Norfolk man, born in 1876 at Rougham, the seat of the younger branch of the North family which owed its origins in the sixteenth century to Edward North, a prominent member of the household of Henry VIII and his Tudor successors. On his mother's side Thomas was related to the Dutch Keppel family who had arrived in England with William of Orange in 1688, shortly after which the Rougham estate was acquired by the family. He was a nephew of Marianne North, the famous Victorian artist, adventurer and philanthropist after whom the Marianne North Gallery in the Royal Botanic Gardens in Kew is named, first opened in 1882.

The young Thomas showed an aptitude for sports, especially field sports with the gun, and at the age of 14 was sent to Uppingham. More practical than academic, on leaving school he departed from the traditional family career path of the law and higher professions in favour of engineering, and entered the Royal Indian Engineering College at Cooper's Hill where he obtained his college diploma and passed the examination for the Indian Civil Service, at the same time winning the trophy for rifle shooting. Instead of moving to some remote corner of the Empire he took up a position as engineer with the Colt Gun Company based in London, but eventually relocated to join the parent company in the United States. In a sense his hobby became his work as he began to collect pistols of all types and built up an unrivalled knowledge of small arms, as well as skill in their intricate repair and renovation. Within the space of a few years he must have acquired a considerable reputation as he was recruited by Vickers Limited in 1913 to take charge of their Works at Crayford in Kent which had fallen into disrepair and disuse, in preparation for the production of small arms. The task ahead was a formidable one, as he was to relate:

'The floors, such as they were, were in many places 18-inches out of level between columns and all the roofs let through the water.'[1]

All this was in sharp contrast to the illustrious history of the plant dating back to 1884 when Sir Hiram Maxim, the American inventor of the automatic machine gun, set up the 'Maxim Gun Company' which turned out large numbers of the weapons for the British Army. In addition Maxim became involved with powered heavier-than-air flight and in 1894 produced and tested a steam-powered flying machine which became airborne (only just) nearly 10 years before the Wright brothers took to the air. However, the technical limitations of the machine put off its financial backers and work on the contraption ceased. In spite of this Sir Hiram deserves a more prominent place in aviation history than has often been recognised and it is only recently that Dartford Council has placed a blue memorial plaque in the town, located at Maypole Primary School in Franklin Road, to commemorate the 1894 flight. In due course Maxim went into partnership with a Sheffield-based armaments company called Vickers & Sons, and in 1911 the company was renamed Vickers Limited, although within a very short time the lack of demand for armaments brought the Works at Crayford to a standstill.

The remit of Thomas North in 1913, starting with a modest work force numbering only about 300, was to prepare the plant and buildings for the production of small arms. The coming of war in 1914 guaranteed a period of very rapid growth in every branch of the armaments industry, and the Vickers Works at Crayford expanded to produce not only small arms but shells for artillery, bayonets, mines and in due course parts for the engines of the newly-invented tank. As Superintendent of the Works, Thomas North presided over this enormous expansion in workload and manpower, combining the roles of inventor, businessman, and manager of a workforce that grew from a few hundred employees in 1913 to 10,000 in 1917, and 12,000 by April 1918 (of which about one-third were women). A world record for the production of thousands of British Elia Mines was claimed, and a tally of over 50,000 Vickers machine guns, tens of thousands of artillery shells and millions of parts for other war materials put Crayford at the forefront of the war effort.

The Vickers Vimy

The Vickers Works at Crayford and Thomas Keppel North will always be associated with the production of the Vickers Vimy, an aircraft immortalised by the first transatlantic flight of 1919.

As early as 1912 the Admiralty had requested that the firm produce a design for an experimental fighting biplane. Thus the buildings at Crayford were extended to include a hangar-like construction called the 'Drome' in which aeroplanes were to be constructed, the first being the FB1 (Fighting Biplane), a two-seater pusher biplane with the propeller behind the wings and a Vickers machine gun mounted in the nose, operated by the observer. The FB5 or Vickers 'Gunbus' as it became known, was delivered to the Royal Flying Corps and was responsible for shooting down a German Taube monoplane on Christmas Day 1914. Two of the aircraft remained at Joyce Green airfield, Dartford, to defend against enemy air attacks on the capital. Such was the pace of technological change that the 'Gunbus' was soon outmatched in combat on the Western Front by the German Fokker aircraft. More successful was the SE5A single-seat fighter which was produced in large numbers at Crayford and was arguably one of the most effective

Vickers Vimy production line at Crayford Works.
(Bexley Local Studies and Archive Centre)

fighters of the war. Other aircraft of the FB series were designed and tested at Crayford and Joyce Green, including the last of the 'pusher' types the FB26 Vampire 2, in which the chief test pilot Harold Barnwell met his death during a test flight at Joyce Green in August 1917. In spite of this setback Thomas North was writing in the Crayford Works Magazine in October 1917 that 'Crayford is the only Works in the world that can turn out a complete aeroplane, with the exception of instruments such as compasses etc, but including the engine and armament of machine and rocket guns.'[2]

As the war progressed the demand for a new generation of heavy bombers culminated in the design of the FB27 which was later to become the Vickers Vimy, named after the Battle of Vimy Ridge in April 1917. The detailed design work for the aircraft was headed by Reginald (Rex) Kirshaw Pierson, chief designer of the company's office located in Knightsbridge, London, who had joined Vickers Ltd in Erith, Kent in 1908 as an engineering apprentice. By coincidence he was also a Norfolk man, born in 1891 and the eldest of four children of Kirshaw Thomas Pierson, rector of Little Fransham. There was no time to lose:

Vickers Gunbus (Bexley Local Studies and Archive Centre)

'Four months after Rex Pierson sketched a rough design of the plane in front of the Air Board at the Hotel Cecil on the Strand, Crayford Superintendent Thomas Keppel North was able to deliver the prototype.'[3]

The first flight took place from the Vickers airfield at Joyce Green on 13 November 1917. Initially the newly-formed Royal Air Force had ordered 1,100 aircraft but this was steadily reduced and with the coming of the Armistice only about 185 had been produced on wartime contracts. Of these about 12 of the bombers were manufactured at Crayford, the main disadvantage of the Works there being that aircraft had to be dismantled and transported by road to Joyce Green. Thus a decision was made to transfer manufacture to Weybridge in Surrey, but the pioneering work was the achievement of the workforce at the Crayford factory under the leadership of Thomas Keppel North.

The Armistice and an unfinished life

The prominence of the Vickers Works at Crayford in war production was recognised by the visit in April 1918 of Queen Alexandra accompanied by the Princess Royal and Princess Maud. As reported in *The Times* of 2 April the royal party were welcomed by Sir Trevor Dawson, managing director of Vickers, Thomas North as Works Superintendent and Major C. S. Paulet from the Ministry of Munitions. Much of the tour was devoted to witnessing machine-gun manufacture with the claim that one complete gun was turned out every five minutes. It is hard to believe that 'the ladies were particularly interested in the methods of truing and inspecting machine-gun barrels' – what they had to do for England! The extent and pace of the work at Crayford was relentless as the war reached its climax during 1918, as North commented:

'If Crayford could be condensed into a single individuality, he or she should immediately make a fortune as a "quick change artiste" at a Variety Show.'[4]

Visit of Queen Alexandra to the Crayford Works in April 1918 accompanied by T. K. North. (Bexley Local Studies and Archive Centre)

Employees at Vickers' Crayford works assemble to celebrate the morning of Armistice Day, 1918

T. K. North at the head of 14,500 Crayford employees on Armistice Day,
11 November 1918. T. K. North stands at the front centre in a light suit.
(Reproduced by permission of Vickers Archives held at Cambridge University Library)

    The Armistice in November 1918 brought to an end the insatiable demand for war equipment, and if only to illustrate the comment of Thomas North, production was switched from machine guns to sewing machines by January 1919. The remaining Vimy bombers had to be dismantled and moved to Weybridge in order to make floor space for the changes, but it remained one of Thomas North's dreams that the Vimy might one day be adapted as a civil airliner. The local newspaper reported that North's one aim when the war ended 'was to transfer with all speed from the manufacture of war material to peace production, in order to help, as far as possible, to minimise the discharge of labour and to prevent human suffering. How hard he struggled to this end is known to few. The many will never be able to know what he attempted on their behalf.' The rapid run-down of the factory was inevitable but in recognition of his wartime achievements

Thomas North was appointed Order of the British Empire (OBE) 'for distinguished services in connection with the output of munitions, explosives, aeroplanes, and other material...and in transforming the Crayford Works from a derelict factory to a great arsenal'.[5]

Within weeks of the war's end Thomas North had succumbed to the deadly 'flu pandemic that claimed so many of his countrymen, and it is open to question how far the excessive workload of the war years weakened his resistance to infection. What was remarkable was the genuine outpouring of grief and sadness at his passing, widely shared within the Works and also in the Crayford community. The Crayford Works Magazine included a poetic tribute from 'a Workman in the Factory' who talked of:

'...the last farewell
To one who in the past six years has proved himself so well.
A Man of honour, aye, indeed. We know we've lost a friend,
Who in his actions ever strove to reach a common end
To raise this place to his ideal, where strife should be debarred;
Where men could work and do their share and not find life press hard...
Whose boast in life was true, we know – "My Word, My Bond." '

An estimated 15,000 workers lined the route of the funeral cortège as it set off for North's birthplace at Rougham in Norfolk, and a memorial service in Crayford Parish Church was held on the same day as the funeral at St Mary's Church in Rougham, 14 February 1919. On his gravestone is carved the image of a Vickers Vimy aeroplane with the wording:

Here lies all that was mortal of Thomas Keppel North OBE, youngest son of the late Charles North of this parish. Who died at Crayford in the County of Kent on the 10th day of February in the year of Our Lord 1919 aged 42 years.

He was the Superintendent of Vickers Works and designed the first aeroplane to cross the ocean.

Seest thou a man diligent in his business? He shall stand before Kings; He shall not stand before mean men. Proverbs XXII 29.

In the succeeding weeks and months many tributes were paid to the work of Thomas North. The local newspaper described the active interest he took in the welfare of the expanding workforce by presiding over works' clubs and institutions and taking pride in the growth of the village and the rapidly growing new housing estate. There was a proposal to raise funds to provide a hospital for the district, dedicated to his memory 'as Mr North's great wish was a hospital for Crayford people'. It is not clear what the

Thomas North's gravestone at St Mary's Churchyard Rougham, Norfolk. The outline of the Vickers Vimy is visible near the top of the stone. (Author)

outcome of this was in the severe economic depression which followed the war, but the episode demonstrated the widespread affection and respect in which he was held.

Within a few weeks, on 23 July, Captain John Alcock and Lieutenant Arthur Whitten Brown came to the Princesses' Theatre in Crayford, the re-building of which after a fire in 1916 had owed much to the intiative of Thomas North, to thank the firm and the workers for building their aircraft because without them 'the flight would not have been made'. The aircraft type went on to become the backbone of the Royal Air Force bomber force for many years as well as being adapted for civil use as the Vimy-Commercial. The design was officially credited to Reginald Kirshaw Pierson, but there was a belief that Thomas North was not given sufficient credit for the achievement in his role as Superintendent of the Works. This may well have been one of the motives behind the legal action of the family against the Vickers Company in 1925, claiming a share of the profits for the wartime work of the company. Perhaps his early death robbed him of the public accolades that were his due. Whatever the rights and wrongs, Thomas Keppel North has an assured place in the annals of aviation history.

Notes:
1 Quoted from a history of the Crayford Works, Kent, in Vickers Archives Doc. No. 621.
2 Ibid.
3 Quoted in *A Magnificent Town and its Flying Machines* by Peter Daniel p 13.
4 Vickers Archives op. cit.
5 *The Times* 15 February 1919.

5

Egbert Cadbury – Zeppelin Hunter

Egbert Cadbury was a night-fighter pilot of the Royal Naval Air Service based at Great Yarmouth, made famous by sharing in the destruction of two enemy Zeppelins.

Egbert ('Bertie') was born in 1893 at Selly Oak in Birmingham, the youngest son of George Cadbury and heir to his father's chocolate empire. After his education at Leighton Park and Trinity College, Cambridge, on the outbreak of war he joined the Royal Navy as an able seaman. He soon decided to join the fledgling Royal Naval Air Service and trained as a pilot at Grahame-White School in Hendon, on the Grahame-White Biplane, obtaining his Royal Aero Club Certificate No. 1343 on 19 June 1915. On 10 July he was commissioned and posted to the naval air station at South Denes, Great Yarmouth.

The air station had its origins in 1912 when the Admiralty opted for a site along the east coast to guard against the German naval threat in the event of war. A narrow five acre strip of land on the shore at South Denes in Yarmouth was chosen, at a low rental which the General Purposes Committee of the Council had fixed at £12 10s per annum. The station was to be used for aeroplanes and seaplanes and was commissioned in April 1913 and at the same time the regional headquarters of what was to become the Royal Naval Air Service was established in the town at Regent Street.

The site, bounded by the River Yare to the west, the harbour mouth to the south and the sea to the east grew rapidly to 85 acres, and by the time war broke out in August 1914 there were four large and several small aircraft sheds with technical and administrative buildings along the beach. There was certainly not a moment to lose because Yarmouth became the first town in England to be bombed from the air on 19 January 1915 by Zeppelin L3 in the first strategic bombing raid of the war. On that night of 19/20 January several other East Anglian villages and towns were hit including Sheringham, Brancaster, Thornham, Hunstanton, Heacham, Snettisham and King's Lynn.

Egbert Cadbury arrived at the station only a few months later and the 22 year-old flight sub-lieutenant was soon engaged in lengthy patrols over the North Sea, often at night, seeking out Zeppelins on their known favoured routes in the direction of East Anglia. Accurate navigation was very difficult for Zeppelins so it was usual for the airships to rendezvous over the Happisburgh lightship, eight miles off the coast at Bacton – sometimes as many as seven or eight craft would do so – then they would cross the coast, sometimes coming over the Wash and heading in the direction of London via King's Lynn, Downham Market, Cambridge and Royston. The air station at Yarmouth was well placed to send out aircraft to intercept.

1343.

CADBURY, Egbert
    Northfield Manor, Birmingham.

Born 20th April 1893. at Selly Oak, Birmingham
Nationality British
Rank or Profession Flight Sub-Lieut.R.N.A.S.
Certificate taken on Grahame-White Biplane
At Grahame-White School, Hendon
Date 19th June, 1915.

Egbert Cadbury's Royal Aero Club Certificate, 19 June 1915
(Reproduced by kind permission of the Royal Aero Club via Andrew Dawrant)

There was usually little to show for these many hours in open cockpits in the freezing cold and with the continual threat of engine or structural failure to contend with, not to mention the danger of 'friendly fire' from our own ships or aircraft. An early opportunity for Cadbury arrived in July 1916 when a Zeppelin was reported near the coast. He was at the Bacton landing ground but was delayed as the aircraft was made ready and by the time he took off to intercept, contact was lost with the airship and mechanical trouble forced him to turn for home. Another disappointment came in September after two and a half hours over the North Sea when he ran short of fuel and returned to Yarmouth, just missing the sighting of a Zeppelin as it crossed his patrol area. To make matters worse, he set off again in the early hours of the morning in a Sopwith Baby seaplane after a Zeppelin had been reported, but once again saw nothing and on his return a minor miscalculation led to the aircraft crashing into the sea and he was lucky to escape with only superficial injuries. Another episode was later described by former Air Mechanic Henry Allingham who occasionally flew with Cadbury on patrols, when they crash-landed on return to the airfield after the nose dipped and half the undercarriage was torn off. They scrambled to safety but not before 'I heard a torrent of expletives from the major [sic] that included words I'd never heard before or since...'.[1]

The next opportunity came on 27 November 1916 when a force of ten airships left their base at Nordholz in Germany to attack targets in

eastern England from Tyneside to East Anglia. One of them, the L34, dropped bombs on West Hartlepool causing damage and several casualties before it was shot down by a Seaton Carew-based BE2c flown by Lt Ian Vernon Pyatt of No. 36 Squadron. Another of the group, L21, dropped bombs on a number of targets in the Midlands before turning south for Norfolk and heading over Yarmouth in the direction of Dereham. The Zeppelin's luck held as she was sighted by a

Flt Sub-Lt E. L. Pulling and Flt Lt E. Cadbury
(www.fengatesroad.com)

fighter but the aircraft's engine failed as it came into the attack. By this time the RNAS pilots at Yarmouth were on full alert and the airship was spotted by Flight Lieutenant Cadbury, and Flight Sub-Lieutenants Gerard Fane and Edward L. Pulling in their BE2cs, as the Zeppelin began to head out to sea for home. Cadbury started the attack from below the Zeppelin at about 700 feet astern and fired off his Lewis gun until he exhausted his ammunition. Fane then moved in but his gun jammed in the frozen air, and now it was Pulling's turn in the face of the now fierce machine-gun fire from the Zeppelin crew. He fired off only two rounds but at this point the Zeppelin burst into flames and crashed in the sea off Lowestoft with no survivors. Pulling was given the main credit for the success and was awarded the DSO while Cadbury and Fane both received the DSC. Sadly Pulling along with a fellow airman Flight Sub-Lieutenant John Northrop were killed in aerobatics over South Denes on 2 March 1917. Both men are buried in Great Yarmouth (Caister) Cemetery.

There was some light relief when Cadbury announced his engagement to a local girl, Mary Phillips, the daughter of the Rev. A. Forbes Phillips, vicar of Gorleston. The wedding took place in a packed Gorleston parish church in February 1917.

As air and ground defences improved Zeppelin raids diminished in the course of 1917 and early 1918 but there was plenty of work for the RNAS airmen to do, patrolling the sea lanes for enemy submarines and other hostile craft. With the formation of the Royal Air Force in April 1918 Cadbury was placed in command of the newly constituted 212 Squadron in the rank of captain. He must have thought his days of Zeppelin-hunting were over but he had not reckoned on the desperate ambition of the commander of the German airship division, Peter Strasser. A new class of airship, the L70, was to lead a force of two others in an almost reckless operation against English targets on Bank Holiday Monday, 5 August 1918. The formation was first sighted off the coast 30 miles north-east of Happisburgh in the light of a summer evening, just at the moment that Cadbury was relaxing to music at a charity concert in which one of the singers was his wife Mary. Not a moment was lost as Cadbury spotted an airship from the seafront, rushed to the airfield and, in the company of Captain Robert Leckie who acted as his gunner on this occasion, took off in a DH4, armed with two bombs which he attempted but failed to jettison, and very soon made visual contact with the airships at about 40 miles distant. The rest of the story is the stuff of aviation legend. At just after 10 o' clock they reached nearly 17,000 feet and Cadbury attacked L70 head-on with explosive bullets sending the airship into a blazing, terminal dive towards the sea. All on board were killed including Strasser, the architect of the Zeppelin war. The next in line was L65 but Leckie's gun jammed and the airship escaped.

The cigarette box made from the Zeppelin shot down by Lt Egbert Cadbury.

Engraved cigarette case of Egbert Cadbury made from Zeppelin L70. (Yarmouth Libraries)

By now pitch blackness had descended and Cadbury had the dangerous task of finding his way through the clouds to a safe landing. Eventually he managed to find landfall at Sedgeford, still with the two bombs on board! Cadbury's heroic exploit marked the end of the Zeppelin offensive and he was recommended for the Victoria Cross, but this was downgraded to a Distinguished Flying Cross, which was also awarded to Robert Leckie.

Cadbury survived the war and became managing director of his father's associate company J. S. Fry and Sons Ltd. During World War II he served as Air Commodore of the City of Bristol Squadron and was knighted in 1957 for public services. He retired as vice-chairman of the Cadbury empire in 1962 and died in Bristol in 1967.

As a footnote to this remarkable life and some years after his death, Egbert's son Peter Cadbury who had been born in Yarmouth in 1918 bought the historic Cromer lifeboat, the H F.Bailey III for £15,000, for permanent display in the town as a tribute to the men who rescued so many of the airmen who had fought alongside his father.

Note:
[1] Quoted in the *Eastern Daily Press* 'Last Salute to a Great Survivor' by Steve Snelling, 25 July 2009. A tribute to Henry Allingham on his death at the age of 113 years.

6

G. S. M. Insall VC – War Hero
and Pioneer of Aerial Archaeology

Gilbert Stuart Martin Insall was a First World War flying hero who later became a pioneer in the use of aerial photography in archaeology.

Early Days

Gilbert Insall was born in Paris on 16 May 1894, the eldest son of Gilbert Jenkins Insall, honorary professor at Ecole Odontotechnique (dentistry). He attended the Anglo-Saxon School in Paris and from an early age was captivated by the emerging craze of pioneering aviation, in which France was the leader at the time. He and his brother Algernon would go to Buc aerodrome at Versailles to watch the Brazilian-born aviator Alberto Santos Dumont who had designed a number of dirigible or steerable-type balloons before moving on to the design and testing of heavier-than-air machines. He made the first public flight of such an aeroplane in October 1906 called *L'Oiseau de proie (bird of prey)*, the first fixed-wing aircraft officially witnessed to take off and land successfully. Later Gilbert Insall watched Santos Dumont's later creation the *Demoiselle (Dragonfly)*, claimed to be the world's first series production aircraft.

Gilbert also watched Louis Blériot in his early flights – an aviator later to make the first successful Channel crossing by a heavier-than-air craft in 1909 – and was able to secure some flights as a passenger with Maurice Farman, who along with his brother Henry were household names in the story of early aviation.

With his inventive turn of mind Gilbert became interested in wireless telegraphy and constructed his own set at home, using his metal bedstead as an aerial. It was through this contraption that he heard about the *Titanic* disaster of April 1912.

At some stage Gilbert enrolled at the Sorbonne University in Paris but along with his brother Algernon went to England on the outbreak of war to enlist as privates in the University and Public Schools Brigade of the Royal Fusiliers, joining the 18th Battalion on 15 September 1914. The brothers spent the months that followed training in London, parading in

Hyde Park and generally biding their time while their applications for the Royal Flying Corps, Military Wing, were being processed by officialdom. Finally the orders came through and the brothers reported on 1 March 1915 to the Military School at Brooklands for flying training.

Flying – at last

At Brooklands the brothers were billeted in the 'Blue Anchor' public house and acquired the nickname 'the Gold-Dust Twins'. Progress was astonishingly rapid, with Gilbert training on a Maurice Farman Biplane, obtaining his Royal Aero Club Certificate No. 1110 on 14 March and the same day being gazetted a second lieutenant (on probation) in the Royal Flying Corps – his brother Algernon had qualified two days earlier. Forty-

Gilbert Insall VC during the First World War.

eight hours' leave was followed by the issue of an officers' kit allowance of £70 and a Colt .455 revolver.

The brothers were posted to Netheravon in April 1915, first to No. 8 Reserve Squadron and then in July to the nucleus of No. 11 Squadron. Algernon was unfortunate to crash while landing and felt unable to continue as a pilot, so he re-mustered as an observer, just in time for the squadron move to France.

Equipped with the Vickers FB5 'The Gunbus' – a pusher biplane with the gunner in the nose (see Chapter 4 on Thomas Keppel North) – the squadron was soon labelled 'The Castor Oil Squadron' as the aircraft tail had to be held down before take-off and the personnel were sprayed with castor oil, with unintended results no doubt.[1]

At last on 25 July the squadron moved to St Omer and by the 29th were in place at Vert Galand, and on the same day flying their first patrol. The work of the squadron varied from photographic reconnaissance to offensive patrolling and 21 year-old Second Lieutenant Gilbert Insall was soon in the thick of the action with his gunner First Class Air Mechanic T. H. Donald, a tough lad who spoke with a broad Scots accent. Air Mechanic (later Sergeant) Joseph Helingoe remembered Gilbert Insall as rather 'domineering and a public-school type' but it was not long before he acquired a reputation as one of the leading pilots on the squadron.[2] On 20 September there was another move, to Villers-Bretonneux and a month later the squadron settled at Bertangles.

Action – and Capture

On 7 November 1915 Insall and Donald set out on a patrol in the Bapaume area and just before they crossed the lines at between 7,000 and 8,000 feet they sighted an enemy kite-balloon used in artillery spotting, and dived towards it hoping to hit it with an incendiary bomb. The attempt failed and in the meantime an enemy two-seater aircraft was heading towards them to intercept. Insall dived into the attack but the enemy manoeuvred to escape, leading Insall over a German rocket battery. Donald was able to fire a complete drum of ammunition before the enemy machine escaped into a cloud and, clearly damaged, descended towards the ground and made a crash landing in a ploughed field, well inside the German lines. The German crew struggled clear but Insall was determined to finish the job and dived towards the crashed aeroplane, finishing it off with the incendiary

**Some First World War
locations in text**

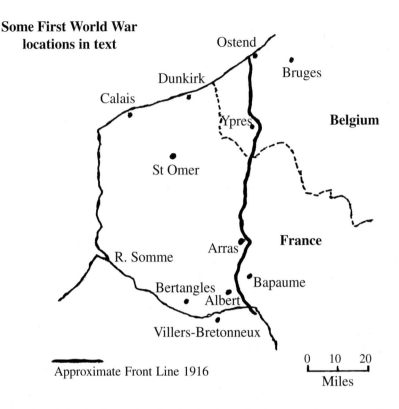

Ostend

Bruges

Dunkirk

Calais

Ypres

Belgium

St Omer

France

R. Somme

Arras

Bertangles

Bapaume

Albert

Villers-Bretonneux

Approximate Front Line 1916

0   10   20
Miles

bomb originally intended for the balloon. In the meantime every German gun in the vicinity had opened up on Insall's machine and he dived to make up speed in the direction of the British lines. The aircraft received multiple hits and by the time it reached no man's land the fuel tank had been punctured and the engine had stopped. Insall was able to bring the aircraft down to a safe landing near the village of Agny, south of Arras and a few hundred yards behind Allied lines, which at that point were in French hands but well within range of German artillery. Overnight the soldiers helped Insall and Donald to make temporary repairs and as dawn broke they just managed to get away, being met as they took off by a hail of machine gun fire from the enemy trenches so that 'all the onlookers (the French soldiers) had to throw themselves flat on the ground, because of the hail of bullets that came cracking through the trees.'[3]

As a result of this exploit Insall was decorated with the Victoria Cross and T. H. Donald the Distinguished Conduct Medal. The squadron was later able to boast another two awards of the VC, to Major Lionel W.

Brabazon Rees in August 1916, and to Albert Ball in 1917 (shortly afterwards to be killed).

Just over a month later, and even before the news of the award of the VC came through from headquarters, Insall's luck ran out and he failed to return from a patrol. Once again with Donald as his gunner he set off on a patrol over Albert, when an enemy aircraft approached them from the direction of Bapaume and combat was joined. The enemy was hit but Donald was wounded in the leg and the engine of the Vickers fighter was put out of action. Insall put the machine into a glide for home lines but by now well over German territory the aircraft was hit by German ack-ack fire which wounded Insall in the left buttock and left no choice but to make a forced landing. They were surrounded by enemy troops and when stretcher-bearers arrived to take away the wounded men, by an incredible coincidence one of them recognised Insall as they had met as rival members of hockey teams before the war, when the Sorbonne Club had travelled to Hanover to play a match with a German team.[4]

Shortly afterwards his brother Algernon received a buff envelope via the Red Cross containing a hand-written note from Gilbert with the information that he was wounded and a prisoner. He was at first held in a Cologne hospital, recovering from his wound, but very soon was planning an escape.

His first escape attempt was made from a military barracks camp at Heidelberg in the company of two other officers. Over many weeks the prisoners had dug a 40-yard tunnel which extended over the perimeter wall and outer wire. They managed to crawl out of the camp but were unable to make any headway in the snow, and sheltered in a woodcutter's cave where they were recaptured. Insall was soon moved to a camp at Krefeld which, at only ten miles from the Dutch frontier, offered an even better escape opportunity. The chance came when the Germans made preparations to move the prisoners to a camp further into Germany to make escape more difficult, and local hauliers were hired to transport packing cases of belongings to the local railway station. Camp orderlies were given the task of loading but Insall and a colleague managed to persuade one of the men to make a space for the two of them to slip into the back of a cart, suitably dressed in casual clothes to hide their uniforms. The guards let the cart through and the two prisoners began their walk through the town to freedom, as they hoped. Unfortunately a suspicious bystander reported them and they were soon recaptured.

By August 1917 Insall and about 800 fellow prisoners were moved to Hanover, to a camp at Ströhen close to what was to become Wunstorf airfield. Never one to give up easily, he spent a period in solitary confinement as punishment, but used the opportunity to plan his next escape attempt. With two colleagues he made a trapdoor and a tunnel towards the floor of an ablutions shed situated outside the wire. The three men hid themselves under the floor of the shed one morning, laid low while the Germans raised the hue and cry, and under cover of nightfall forced their way out of the shed and after a trek of nine hours reached the Dutch frontier near Venlo and freedom. The date was 28 August, some 20 months after Insall had been taken prisoner. In recognition of his daring escape he was decorated with the Military Cross. Some 37 years later Group Captain Gilbert Insall, at that time the oldest surviving VC holder of the RAF, was flown to Wunstorf to watch the Presentation of the Royal Standard to his former No. 11 Squadron and immediately recognised the camp site from which he had escaped, which by then had become a rifle range.

Aerial Photographer and Archaeologist

Gilbert Insall's skill in digging tunnels for escape as a prisoner of war allegedly encouraged him in a new passion, archaeological excavation. This interest had been kindled by his experiences in photographic reconnaissance during the war when he began to realise the potential of spotting landmarks from the air which were invisible at ground level. He obtained a permanent commission in the newly formed Royal Air Force in the rank of squadron leader, and served in a number of training posts before resuming operational flying.

In August 1924 he was based at No. 1 Flying Training School at Netheravon in Wiltshire on Salisbury Plain as an administrative officer and took every opportunity to fly over an area rich in ancient sites. During the winter of 1925 he was flying near Amesbury, about two miles from Stonehenge, and at about two thousand feet sighted a large circular earthwork with a series of concentric white marks within it in a ploughed field. This site had been known previously to antiquarians but never before properly understood. Insall flew over the site again the following June in a Sopwith Snipe to take an aerial photograph and found the field fully in wheat with the unusual features appearing dark against the lighter background. Later investigation proved that these were the traces of timber circles and datable to the Bronze Age, an important discovery which was named Woodhenge, believed to be a wooden version of the nearby Stonehenge. The find brought Insall into contact with O. G. S. Crawford, the first Archaeology Officer of Ordnance Survey, who did everything he could to encourage young archaeologists 'to join a flying club and learn to fly'.[5] Crawford publicised some of these and later developments in *Antiquity*, a quarterly review of archaeology that he founded in 1927. Volume I of the journal included extracts from a letter written by Insall (now based in Basra) describing what he photographed at Woodhenge from the air and concluded 'I climbed on to a hayrick in the same field a few days later, and although a few dark patches could be seen in the standing wheat, no pattern was visible, and they would have passed unnoticed. From the air the details of the site were as clear as shown on the photograph, if not clearer.'

During 1926 Insall married Olwen Scott, daughter of J. A. Yates, but very soon his next posting came through, to Basra in Iraq in September 1926 for air staff duties at the RAF station. Iraq, or more accurately Mesopotamia, had been allocated to Britain as a mandated territory on the break-up of the Ottoman Empire at the end of the Great War. The following April he joined No. 70 (Bomber) Squadron as a flight commander based at Hinaidi, also in Iraq, which had the task of subduing dissident tribesmen in the south of the territory. Insall's work with the squadron during 1927 and 1928 earned him a Mention in Despatches, but he also used whatever opportunities presented themselves to search out historic sites in that most ancient of landscapes. By means of aerial photographs he was able to trace the course of the 'Median Wall' built between the Rivers Tigris and Euphrates near Habbaniyah to the north of the ancient city of Babylon and believed to date back to the reign of Nebuchadnezzar II in the 6th Century BC. O. G. S. Crawford took the chance to visit the area in 1928-9 and was flown by Insall over the ancient Kingdom of Seleucia in Mesopotamia, and rapturously observed the site of the city of Hatra, said to be the capital of the first Arab Kingdom in Mesopotamia which had flourished at the time of Christ and had resisted Roman conquest.[6]

Returning to England in early March 1929, Insall was appointed to command the newly re-formed No. 35 (Bomber) Squadron based at Bircham Newton, equipped at first with the de Havilland DH9A and later the Fairey IIIF. His interest was drawn to the rich archaeological heritage of Norfolk revealed by a succession of air photographs, for example of the Roman town of Caistor-by-Norwich, or Caistor St Edmund, three miles south-east of Norwich. The site had been known previously but there had been some debate as to whether this was the *Venta Icenorum* (the centre of the Iceni) rather than Norwich but a local saying that 'Caistor was a city when Norwich was none' seemed to confirm its importance. The Roman town was thought to have been established after Boudicca's rebellion of AD 60/61 and built over the Iceni tribal settlement to become a regional capital in Roman Britain. For the first time RAF aerial photographs from 1928 revealed the network of streets and buildings which enabled archaeologists to plan a series of excavations. Accordingly an excavation committee was formed by the Norfolk and Norwich Archaeological Society and six seasons of excavation took place between 1929 and 1935 under the direction of the Roman town scholar Professor Donald Atkinson. Some 80 years later in 2009 and 2010 archaeologists have returned to the site in a new Caistor Project under the direction of Dr Will Bowden of the University of Nottingham.[7]

Gilbert Insall was well aware of the discoveries connected with Caistor and was closely involved from the beginning, but one day in June

Caistor-by-Norwich (Caistor St Edmund) Roman Camp – Venta Icenorum
Photo taken by RAF 10 August 1928. (English Heritage. NMR Crawford Collection)

1929 he was flying south-east from the city of Norwich along the Tas valley, known as an area rich in prehistoric sites, and he made a remarkable discovery. He sighted traces of two concentric circles, one within the other, associated with several dark specks in a horseshoe-shaped pattern. Realising that this was no random image but clearly something significant, he returned to take a photograph from the air on 18 June 1929 from a height of about 4,000 feet which confirmed the patterns he had witnessed. O. G. S. Crawford visited the site a week later and pronounced it to be the Norwich Woodhenge, but it was to be six years before the 'Arminghall Henge', as it became known, was excavated by Grahame Clark, later Professor of Archaeology at Cambridge. The site was found to be a ritual enclosure dating to the late Neolithic period, some 3000 BC, with the 'specks' turning out to be the postholes of oak timbers set out together with mounds and ditches, making it one of the most important prehistoric discoveries up to that time, and comparable with the recent Holme-next-the-Sea henge discovery in 1999.[8]

Insall had little time to reflect on these developments as he was promoted to the rank of wing commander and appointed station commander

'Arminghall Henge', near Norwich. Photo taken by Gilbert Insall 18 June 1929.
(English Heritage. NMR Crawford Collection)

at Donibristle in July 1929. Further station commands followed at Upavon in July 1932 and Kenley in May 1934. He was based at Heliopolis in Egypt in 1935, now as a group captain, and it must have been during his overseas posting that he 'took the first ever clear pictures from the air through clear water of Cleopatra's Baths near Aboukir'.[9]

Retiring from the RAF in 1945 Insall took up field archaeology as a full-time occupation. He settled in Scrooby, near Bawtry, Nottinghamshire, where he purchased a house called 'Monks Hill' and from there organised more than 200 field surveys throughout the country for the then Ministry of Works which greatly assisted future archaeologists. He died in February 1972 at the age of 77. The funeral service took place in Bawtry and the *Doncaster Evening Post* of 24 February reported that the township was brought to a standstill in honour of 'one of Britain's first fighter pilots'. Police halted the traffic and hundreds of people lined the route as the RAF procession led by the RAF Regiment band and an open Land Rover carrying the coffin wound its way from Bawtry Hall to the parish church half a mile away. Cremation followed in Doncaster. Insall is commemorated with a

*Graves of Gilbert Insall VC and his wife in the churchyard of
All Saints, Nocton, Lincolnshire.*

headstone in Nocton Churchyard, Lincolnshire. His Victoria Cross is displayed at the Royal Air Force Museum in Hendon and he is named on a memorial in the Royal Air Force Church, St Clement Danes, London.

Gilbert Insall's place in history would have been secure as only the fifth pilot to be awarded the Victoria Cross and by the remarkable escape from captivity which earned him a Military Cross. But his spectacular achievements in the ground-breaking technique of aerial photography marks him out as an exceptional aviator. First employed over the battlefields of the First World War, aerial photography opened a new window on the landscape with far-reaching consequences for the understanding of our physical environment, and future generations owe a debt to people like Gilbert Insall for meeting its challenges.

Notes:

[1] Joseph Helingoe (Observer No. 11 Sqn RFC) – reminiscences (recorded on CD 25 March 1976 – RAF Museum).
[2] Ibid.
[3] Insall, A. J., *Observer: Memoirs of the RFC 1915-18* pp 110-102.
[4] Ibid. p104.
[5] Hauser, Kitty, *Bloody Old Britain: O. G. S. Crawford and the Archaeology of Modern Life*, p 83.
[6] Deuel, Leo, *Flights into Yesterday*, p111.
[7] *Eastern Daily Press* Reports 26 August 2009 and 28 August 2010..
[8] *Eastern Daily Press* Magazine 24 July 1999, article by Steve Snelling, 'How traces of history marked an aerial milestone.'
[9] Info from notes supplied by Peter Elliott, RAF Museum Library.

7

Nevil Shute (Nevil Shute Norway) – Aeronautical Engineer and Novelist

Early Days

Nevil Shute was an aeronautical engineer who became one of the world's best-selling novelists during the 1950s and 1960s. In his writing career he wrote at least 24 novels, of which around six were box-office successes as films. Born in Ealing in 1899, son of Arthur Hamilton Norway CB and Mary Louisa Gadsden, he received a conventional middle-class education at Shrewsbury. His father was at that time head of the post office in Dublin in 1916 and Nevil witnessed at first hand the Easter Rising, even being commended for his work as a stretcher bearer. In his spare time Arthur Norway had been in the habit of writing local travel books, a fact that was probably not lost on the young Nevil.

The family suffered a heavy blow in 1915 when his brother Fred was killed in the war but Nevil opted to join the Royal Flying Corps and

passed into the Royal Military Academy at Woolwich in 1918. However, he failed the medical due to a severe stammer which stayed with him for most of his life. Instead he enlisted as a private in the Suffolk Regiment, serving out much of the last year of the war in the Isle of Grain at the mouth of the Thames. At the end of 1918 he was detailed to act as a clerk assisting in the task of demobilisation at Shorncliffe Camp near Folkestone and in the course of his duties discovered one or two aircraft left derelict in a hangar, an opportunity for him to use his off-duty hours sitting in the cockpit of a Sopwith Camel familiarising himself with the instruments and controls, and the distinctive oily smell. The experience must have convinced him of his future vocation.

Nevil Shute in 1949, at the height of his fame as a novelist.

Aeronautical Engineer

After his army service he was accepted for Balliol College, Oxford, to read engineering where amongst other things he discovered a passion for sailing. Towards the end of his time at Oxford an introduction was secured to the Aircraft Manufacturing Company at Hendon (Airco) and Nevil began work there in the design office, at first unpaid, but gaining valuable experience. The work at Airco began to wind down with the years of peace and he then took up the opportunity to join the de Havilland Aircraft company which was in the process of becoming established. An early acquaintance was Alan Cobham, who had just joined the organisation as a pilot.

When the company established a flying school Nevil decided to learn to fly but this was at the considerable cost of five pounds ten shillings per hour, which meant that he had to rely partly on parental support in the venture. However, success came with the award of Royal Aero Club Certificate No. 7954 on 4 March 1924.

With few distractions in the evenings he also began to write, completing two novels neither of which were accepted for publication and were therefore shelved but the 'bug' had bitten. The fact that he was serious about writing at this time is illustrated by a letter he wrote in April 1923 to the Society of Authors from his address at Stag Lane in Edgware, requesting election to the Society and enclosing a cheque for the fee of one pound ten pence. In support of his application he added that aviation had often been the butt of novelists but had never before been treated in novel form 'by one who knows it intimately from the inside'.[1]

Late in 1924 Nevil left de Havillands due to the lack of promotion prospects, and joined Vickers Ltd as Chief Calculator under the leadership of Barnes Wallis. The main task was to work on the R100 airship project which began in Vickers House, Westminster, and then for more than a year 'in a derelict office in the depressing industrial suburb of Crayford in Kent'[2] (see also chapter 4). By 1926 the preliminary work on the airship was completed and the Vickers team moved north to Howden in Yorkshire to begin the construction. The project was successful but remained in the shadow of its government-sponsored rival the R101 based at Cardington, right up to the point of the fatal crash of the latter at Beauvais in France in October 1930, with the loss of 48 lives including the Secretary of State for Air Lord Thomson. The disaster was a major factor in the decision to ground and eventually scrap the R100, although this craft had more than proved its worth in trials. The background to the tragedy bears comparison with the explosion of Nimrod XV230 in September 2006 over Afghanistan with the loss of 14 lives, characterised by a similar level of official bungling and mistakes over flight safety issues. Disillusioned by the experience of the R100 episode, Nevil was to harbour a lasting suspicion and resentment of government bureaucracy and incompetence which in his view had contributed to the R101 catastrophe and the consequent collapse of airship development.

Airspeed

Nevil's work had dried up, but on the positive side he was convinced of the future of light aircraft manufacturing so with a few trusted colleagues he left Vickers to found a new company called Airspeed Ltd with capital of £1,000, all he had to his name, in the modest premises of an old garage in York. In the economic depression of the early 1930s it was an uphill task to raise sufficient capital to get started but Nevil was able to attract the support of a number of influential figures including Sir Alan Cobham, recently knighted for his pioneering flights around the world.

The company, small scale by the standards of the day, struggled from the start with a shortage of capital and ever increasing overdraft, but succeeded in producing the first of a series of civil aircraft in the Airspeed Ferry in 1932 and the Courier which emerged in 1933. Nevil, as joint managing director, took the next step in negotiating a public issue of shares and the relaunch of the company as Airspeed (1934) Ltd, with headquarters now based in Portsmouth and a workforce soon to be numbered in the hundreds.

Work proceeded apace during 1934. The Airspeed Envoy was developed from the Courier as a small and economical passenger-carrying civil aircraft which promised international appeal as well as interest from the Air Ministry. Towards the end of 1936 this was translated into orders for the Envoy, later to be re-named the Airspeed Oxford and to become the standard Royal Air Force twin-engined training aircraft used throughout the British Commonwealth during the war. As the orders flowed in, Nevil found some spare time to resume his writing career with the publication of *Ruined City* and the sale of the film rights of *Lonely Road* to Ealing Studios. A notable order for the Envoy came from the recently established King's Flight in March 1937 for the personal use of King George VI and the

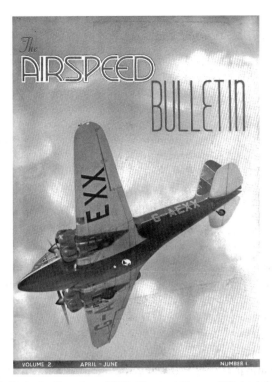

Airspeed Bulletin April to June 1937, Airspeed Envoy. (Flightglobal Archive)

Airspeed Envoy at Bircham Newton, c. 1937.

OPERATIONS RECORD BOOK

See instructions for use of this form, in K.R. and A.C.I., para. 2340, and War Manual, Pt.II., chapter XX., and notes in R.d.F. Pocket Book.

of (Unit or Formation) R.A.F. STATION BIRCHAM NEWTON

No. of pages used for day..............

Place.	Date.	Time.	Summary of Events.	References to Appendices.
Bircham Newton	29.8.39		(Continued) Their Royal Highnesses left by air in an Air Speed Envoy G/AEXX piloted by Wing Commander Luidlaw. A.F.C. M.O. (Captain of the Kings Flight) for Barkston at 1515 hours.	
do	20.8.39		A state of Emergency in the Royal Air Force inaugurated.	
do	1.9.39		General Mobilization of the Royal Air Force was ordered by the Air Council by Signal X877, time of origin 1620 hrs.	
do	3.9.39		A state of War was declared to exist between Great Britain and Germany as from 1100 hours of this date.	

Extract from RAF Bircham Newton Operations Record Book, August 1939.

Nevil Shute as Lt-Cdr (RNVR)
(John Anderson & Nevil Shute Norway Foundation)

Royal Family, which would be the largest aeroplane as yet acquired for that role. The King's Flight had been formed in July 1936 but Edward VIII had abdicated in December of that year and had sold his personal Dragon Rapide which had been used on some of his official engagements, leaving the Duke of York, now King but without any official air transport. It was therefore decided to make available public funds for the first time to purchase an aircraft. Thus, the Captain of the King's Flight, Wing Commander (later Air Vice-Marshal) Edward H. Fielden personally inspected the Envoy, resplendent in its colourful Brigade of Guards finish. Nevil was somewhat sceptical at first of the need to provide extra seating for a steward in flights that would probably not exceed more than two or three hours. But 'in explanation I received a brief account of the fatigue that royal personages must endure, a disturbing picture of people who had shaken a thousand hands smiling and waving to the crowd as they got into the aeroplane and collapsing in a coma of fatigue, grey-faced and utterly exhausted.'[3] The Envoy G-AEXX was a familiar sight in various royal flights until the start of the war and was frequently seen in hangars at Bircham Newton, conveniently close to the royal residence of Sandringham House.

By 1938 Nevil felt that it was time to leave the company, having presided over its growth from modest beginnings to an enterprise with orders worth £1.2 million and a workforce of over a thousand. With all the talk of war there was the prospect of a full order book for years to come. He felt the time had come to concentrate on family life and further novel writing (he had married Frances Mary Heaton in 1931). There was little respite before the country was once again plunged into war, and Nevil found himself commissioned as a sub-lieutenant in the Royal Naval Volunteeer Reserve for work on weapons research as consultant to Sir Dennis Burney, a former boss of Vickers. His skill and experience as an aeronautical engineer was first put to use in the development and testing of gliding torpedoes or Toraplanes, requiring liaison between air force and navy personnel.

The Snapper Incident: Did fact become fiction?

In the meantime two novels were published during 1940, *An Old Captivity* and *Landfall: A Channel Story*. The latter is the story of a young Anson pilot called Jerry Chambers in Coastal Command, based at a fictional aerodrome on the south coast, near Portsmouth. In the course of a patrol in the English Channel (precisely dated 3 December 1939) in search of an enemy U-Boat which has sunk a merchant ship, Chambers and his crew sight a submarine, and believing it to be the German U-Boat, attack and sink it. When they return to the aerodrome Chambers is accused of sinking a Royal Navy submarine which has failed to return to base. In an effort to redeeem his reputation he is posted to an experimental weapons unit and is later seriously injured in an explosion, but survives to be decorated for bravery. The story ends happily, with Chambers vindicated in the knowledge that the submarine he sank was, after all, a German one.

This story highlights the many difficulties in those early months of the war of providing an effective response to the German submarine threat as boats would try to slip through the North Sea into the Atlantic where they would wreak havoc with our convoys. Aerial observation was crucial in locating and destroying the enemy boats but the main equipment of Coastal Command, the Avro Anson, had a limited range of just over 500 miles with two 100lb bombs and the crew was forced to rely on visual recognition at low level to identify possible targets. There seems to be strong circumstantial evidence that Nevil drew on his own knowledge of actual events during those early months of the war to construct the plot of *Landfall*, as outlined by John Anderson in his article 'The Snapper Incident'. Did fact become fiction?

Sunday 3 December 1939 was a calm and clear day and Anson K6184 VX-P of No. 206 Squadron took off from Bircham Newton at 0715 hrs for a routine North Sea patrol to search for enemy ships and submarines. The crew of four consisted of the captain Pilot Officer Henderson (navigator) and Pilot Officer R. H. Harper (pilot) along with air gunner Aircraftman Pugh and wireless operator Aircraftman Williamson. At about 1020 hrs off the coast of Holland and 150 miles out from base a submarine was sighted on the surface at about eight miles distant. On approach from about 1,500

Montgolfier balloon c. 1800 in Tivoli Gardens, Paris.

James Deeker, the first man to fly in Norfolk, ascends from Quantrell's Gardens Norwich, 1 June 1785 (from a painting by John Constable Reeve, Norfolk & Suffolk Aviation Museum)

*Artist's impression of the bombing of Snettisham on the night of 19 January 1915
by Zeppelin L4. (Reproduced by permission of Ben Mullarkey (artist) and
Hugh Mullarkey, who commissioned the painting)* See over the page for memorial

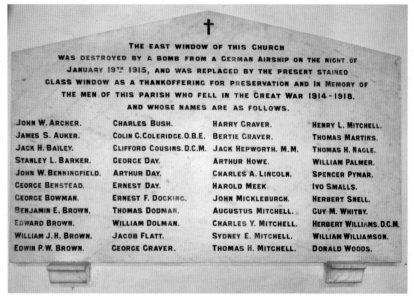

THE EAST WINDOW OF THIS CHURCH
WAS DESTROYED BY A BOMB FROM A GERMAN AIRSHIP ON THE NIGHT OF
JANUARY 19TH 1915, AND WAS REPLACED BY THE PRESENT STAINED
GLASS WINDOW AS A THANKOFFERING FOR PRESERVATION AND IN MEMORY OF
THE MEN OF THIS PARISH WHO FELL IN THE GREAT WAR 1914-1918.
AND WHOSE NAMES ARE AS FOLLOWS.

JOHN W. ARCHER.	CHARLES BUSH.	HARRY CRAVER.	HENRY L. MITCHELL.
JAMES S. AUKER.	COLIN C. COLERIDGE. O.B.E.	BERTIE CRAVER.	THOMAS MARTINS.
JACK H. BAILEY.	CLIFFORD COUSINS. D.C.M.	JACK HEPWORTH. M.M.	THOMAS H. NAGLE.
STANLEY L. BARKER.	GEORGE DAY.	ARTHUR HOWE.	WILLIAM PALMER.
JOHN W. BENNINGFIELD.	ARTHUR DAY.	CHARLES A. LINCOLN.	SPENCER PYMAR.
GEORGE BENSTEAD.	ERNEST DAY.	HAROLD MEEK	IVO SMALLS.
GEORGE BOWMAN.	ERNEST F. DOCKING.	JOHN MICKLEBURGH.	HERBERT SNELL.
BENJAMIN E. BROWN.	THOMAS DODMAN.	AUGUSTUS MITCHELL.	GUY M. WHITBY.
EDWARD BROWN.	WILLIAM DOLMAN.	CHARLES Y. MITCHELL.	HERBERT WILLIAMS. D.C.M.
WILLIAM J.H. BROWN.	JACOB FLATT.	SYDNEY E. MITCHELL.	WILLIAM WILLIAMSON.
EDWIN P.W. BROWN.	GEORGE CRAVER.	THOMAS H. MITCHELL.	DONALD WOODS.

First World War Memorial in Snettisham Church. The Church was claimed to be the first church in England to have been hit by a German bomb during a Zeppelin raid. It was dropped in the field as shown in the picture (see previous page) and most of the windows on the south and east sides of the church were shattered and other damage was done to the fabric.

May your Christmas be Free From raids

World War One Christmas Card.

'Triumphs of the Air'. A post card advertising Shell petrol and quoting the record-breaking first flight between London and Manchester by French aviator Louis Paulhan on 28 April 1910.

Cartoon of the 1910 General Election following Lloyd George's 'People's Budget' of 1909 which introduced taxes for the wealthy. The Liberal Government lost more than 150 seats, ending up with the same number as the Conservatives and the Irish put together. Liberal ministers tumbling from the aeroplane include Herbert Asquith (Prime Minister) and Lloyd George (Chancellor) in the foreground. A young Winston Churchill is in the background. (Details supplied by Professor John Charmley).

A formation of aircraft of Cobham's Flying Circus:
Foreground: red Avro 504 G-EBIZ of the Cornwall Aviation Company Ltd founded by
Capt. Percival Phillips which joined Cobham's National Aviation Day during the 1930s.
Top left yellow Southern Martlet G-ABBN. Top right Cierva Autogyro G-ABGB.
Foot of page Handley-Page W.10 G-EBMR 'Giant Airliner'.
(Reproduced from Aeromodeller *Dec 1949: artist C. Rupert Moore)*

Cobham badge allegedly given to those who had looped the loop with Cobham's Flying Circus. (David Lloyd-Jones).

 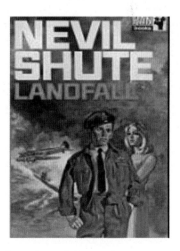

Landfall: *two paperback versions of the novel (John Anderson & Nevil Shute Norway Foundation)*

Poster advertising British Hospitals' Air Pageant in King's Lynn, 2 August 1933.

Alex Henshaw with Henry Labouchere and the DH Leopard Moth

Henry Labouchere with the historic Gypsy Moth G-AAXG.

Poster advertising the 'Wallbro' Centenary at
Norfolk and Suffolk Aviation Museum, 4 July 2010

Wallis type WA–116 (XR–943) Autogyro 'Little Nellie'.

Reg. Even "Little Nellie" has carried a variety of cameras, mostly cine', up to 70 m.m. 'Arriflex'.

Best wishes

Ken

Wallis type WA-116 (XR-943) Autogyro 'Little Nellie' = 007!

*'Little Nellie': Wallis type WA-116 (XR-943) Autogyro,
one of three military type WA-116 built in 1962. The aircraft pictured
as seen in the James Bond film* You Only Live Twice. *(Ken Wallis)*

Replica rockets and other materials from the James Bond film. (Ken Wallis)

Ken Wallis at the Norfolk and Suffolk Aviation Museum, 4 July 2010. (author)

East Anglian
Air Ambulance

Use instructions for use of this form in K.R. and A.C.I.,
para 2349, and War Manual, Pt. II., chapter XX., and
note in R.A.F. Pocket Book.

OPERATIONS RECORD BOOK

R.A.F. Form 540

of (Unit or Formation)......206 SQUADRON......

No. of pages used for day..........

BIRCHAM NEWTON 3–12–39		
	06.50	SEVEN AIRCRAFT. of attacked "B" F. (PATROL) at HORTON PARK Transglove T(+9) in motion to 003 degrees. (B) This machines to SKROTH Pt. The Royalds down are Martians party move to SKROTH Pts. HOOTON PARK for facing on HUDSON aircraft.
		TWO AIRCRAFT engaged on lowry late until 13.35 L.A. with NORTH BOUND convoy. No enemy seen. Weather throughout day. Fine with good visibility until evening when it closed to 1500 yards
	07.16	ONE AIRCRAFT engaged at one hourly intervals on road in vicinity of HAAKS. MAAS L.T. Vessel.
		ANSON K6184. PILOT. P/o HARPER WITT NAVIGATOR. P/o HENDERSON 40126 (CAPT.) W/Op. A/C. WILLIAMSON Mk. Nk. PUGH. notes on patrol at hrs about 150 miles out sighted an enemy submarine on the surface.
		P/o HARPER approached out of the sun and carried out a successful dive bombing attack. ONE 100 LB. bomb dropped and seen to hit submarine at the base of the coning tower. Large oil patch and with small amount of wreckage.
		see attached report and photograph

65

No. 206 Squadron Operations Record Book extract, 3 December 1939, reporting attack on submarine.

– 96 –

Avro Anson on patrol in the North Sea, c. 1939/40.

feet Harper made a complete circuit and, seeing no recognition signals or distinctive markings, assumed it to be an enemy U-Boat (later reported as a U 37 class). As the submarine began a crash dive Harper decided to attack out of the sun and dropped one 100lb bomb which, according to the squadron operations record book, was reported to have hit and exploded at the base of the conning tower followed by a large spreading oil slick 'and bubbles appeared with a small amount of wreckage'[4]. On return to Bircham Newton Harper was in no doubt that they had sunk an enemy submarine and made an official report to that

Highly optimistic impression of Avro Anson sinking a submarine.
(Aeroplane 29 March 1940)

effect. Given the fact that anti-submarine warfare was anything but an exact science at the time there could be no confirmation of the sinking, but within days doubts began to emerge when the captain of a Royal Navy submarine HMS *Snapper*, Lieutenant William King, reported an attack by an aircraft off the coast of Holland on the same day (3 December) and very close to the actual time (1016 hrs) of Harper's attack. Two bombs (not one) were reported to have exploded but no serious damage was caused. However, the distance between the reported locations of Harper's attack and that on *Snapper* was approximately 20 miles. When *Snapper* returned to base at Harwich Lieutenant King read the reports of the attack by the Coastal Command Anson and the naval authorities began to put two and two together, although no record of this attack was included in the Admiralty report.

If one discounts the possibility that an enemy aircraft was in the vicinity at the same time as the Anson, the circumstantial evidence at least supports the theory that HMS *Snapper* was mistakenly attacked by Harper. There are close parallels between the *Snapper* incident and the story in *Landfall*. Although the location in the novel is the English Channel and not the North Sea, the date is the same (3 December) and there was an Anson squadron, No. 48 (GR), based at Thorney Island in Hampshire, near the

HMS *Snapper leaving Malta harbour for England in 1939,*
as she would have been painted in December 1939 i.e. black.
(John Anderson & Nevil Shute Norway Foundation)

location of the fictional Anson squadron. Moreover, Nevil was closely involved with weapons development as a member of the Toraplane and Doravane Development Committee (TDD Committee) under the chairmanship of Admiral Sir William Jones, the Commander-in-Chief Portsmouth. Nevil attended the fourth meeting of the committee on 12 December 1939 at Admiralty House in Portsmouth, only days after the *Snapper* affair. Senior naval and air force officers were present including Air Commodore T. B. Howe, Air Officer Commanding 17 Group Coastal Command. It is likely that the affair was discussed along with the continuing problems of co-ordination between naval and air patrols. There was no secret that the Royal Navy sought control over RAF Coastal Command.

The problem of mistaken identity in submarine recognition was not new. The difficulties facing aircrews were immense even in almost perfect weather conditions. On 5 September 1939 an Anson of No. 233 Squadron with Pilot Officer G. J. D. Yorke at the controls, based at RAF Leuchars, was on the return leg of a patrol and sighted a submarine. Calculating that it was an enemy, the entire bomb load was dropped and damage was reported to the vessel. The crew then resumed the course for home but shrapnel holes in the wing tanks of the aircraft was causing the fuel to drain away and they were forced to ditch in the Eden estuary. The crew managed to scramble to a dinghy and were soon rescued. The riotous celebrations in the Mess that night were brought to an abrupt close when it was learned from the Admiralty that the bombs had hit HMS *Seahorse*, causing little damage. Sadly the submarine met its end on 7 January 1940 in the North Sea, presumed to be the victim of enemy depth charging.

On the same day, 5 September, a 206 Squadron aircraft reported attacking a submarine 85 miles north-east of Lowestoft, without damage being reported. On 27 September Pilot Officer R. C. Patrick of 206 Squadron reported to his commanding officer 'a successful attack' on a submarine near Lundy Island while on detachment at Carew Cheriton in Pembrokeshire. He reported a large patch of bubbles and two irregular patches of oil appearing on the surface, but there was no confirmation that this was a 'kill' or the conclusive identity of the submarine – it may indeed have been a U-Boat. The confidence and heroic efforts of the Anson crews was a triumph of optimism over harsh experience as the armament they carried, two 100lb bombs, were hopelessly inadequate even with a direct hit and were alleged to do little more than 'rattle the teacups'[5]. There was no proper bombsight which meant an attack had to be conducted at very low level, which put the Anson in danger of one of its own bombs exploding in the air. Even the 250lb bomb later used by flying boats had to explode within six feet of the pressure hull for any serious damage to result.[6] It would be rash to claim that an Anson *never* sunk a U-Boat, but in spite of the bravery of the Anson crews the first confirmed U-Boat sinking for which credit could be claimed by an RAF aircraft was on 30 January 1940 when a Sunderland of No. 228 Squadron attacked and damaged U-55 so severely that the crew were forced to scuttle the boat as naval ships closed in.[7] In any case the Anson was soon being phased out in the role by the Lockheed Hudson, an altogether more effective offensive aircraft.

The plot of *Landfall* has many parallels with the *Snapper* incident and it would have been in keeping with Nevil Shute's style to base his stories on personal experience, as with many of his other novels. The book was made into a film in 1948 starring Michael Denison. Nevil Shute Norway later rose to the rank of lieutenant-commander (RNVR) and continued to be involved in weapons development and in novel writing. Pilot Officer Harper was awarded the Distinguished Flying Cross in February 1940, but this was as a result of his bombing of a Dornier Do18 on the water early in 1940. Later he was to become a squadron leader and one of the longest-serving pilots on 206 Squadron until tragedy struck on 2 December 1944 when his Liberator caught fire and crashed in the sea off Crail, on the coast of Fife. No trace of the aircraft was ever found and Harper and his crew are commemorated on the Runnymede Memorial to the Missing. HMS *Snapper* also came to a sad end, disappearing off the Bay of Biscay under the command of Lieutenant Prowse (King was absent on sick leave at the time), the victim either of a minefield or German warships.

Nevil Shute was to become one of the world's best selling novelists during the 1950s and 1960s. Disillusioned with life in Britain, he emigrated to Australia after the war and completed at least ten of his most memorable novels with an Australian theme including *A Town like Alice* (1950) and possibly the most famous of all *On the Beach* (1957). He died in Melbourne in 1960 but his memory is kept alive by his many devoted readers to this day in the Nevil Shute Foundation. Also, in 2009 Vintage Books reprinted many of his titles, demonstrating Nevil Shute's enduring appeal as a novelist in the 21st century.

Notes:

1 British Library, Nevil Shute Norway correspondence (Add MS 56763).
2 Shute, Nevil, *Slide Rule*, p58.
3 Ibid. p216.
4 RAF Form 540 (206 Squadron Operations Record Book).
5 A quote from the late Wing Commander J. C. Graham, who flew Liberators with 206 Squadron later in the war.
6 Terraine, J., *Business in Great Waters* p248 and note 18 pp 701-2.
7 Price, A., *Aircraft Versus Submarine* p46.

8

Alan Cobham and the Barnstormers, Joy-riders and Circus Flyers

'Fly anyone - anywhere'

The Great War had produced an expansion of air power and on both sides of the Atlantic there were surplus pilots and aero engineers whose services were suddenly no longer required. Military aeroplane manufacture took up every available square foot of factory space as the switch began to peacetime production. As always in wartime there had been undreamed of technological advances and for aeroplanes this meant increased engine power, speed, range, carrying capacity and reliability.

Wartime restrictions in civil flying were lifted by early 1919 and this presented an opportunity to meet the fresh challenges – a perfect example being the record-breaking flight in June 1919 across the Atlantic

Farmer. "DEAR ME! C-CAN I DO ANYTHING?"
Airman. "THANKS, BUT REALLY I THINK I'VE DONE ALL THERE IS TO BE DONE."

A Punch cartoon of 1920.

by Captain John Alcock and Lieutenant Arthur Whitten Brown in the Vickers Vimy, originally designed as a bomber but now adapted for long-distance endurance (see Chapter 4).

A more light-hearted approach was adopted by the so-called 'Barnstormers' and 'Circus flyers' – terms imported from across the Atlantic to describe individual stunt pilots who flew throughout the country selling aeroplane flights, often operating from farmers' fields for a day or two before moving on. The so-called 'Barnstorming season' started from early spring and took in the harvest and country fair season until autumn with pilots sometimes organising themselves in groups or 'circuses' to provide more of a spectacle for the crowds.

One of the first on the scene was a company called A. V. Roe and Co. Ltd which assembled a fleet of Avro 504Ks to fly to holiday resorts like Blackpool, Southport and Weston-super-Mare offering half a crown or five shilling 'joy-rides' or 'flips'. It proved a success as around 30,000 passengers were carried. Also in 1919 a young aviator called Alan John Cobham was fresh out of flying school and eager to take up the challenge. Born in 1894 he had joined the army in 1914 and became a sergeant in the Veterinary Corps, skilled in the treatment of horses. From this unlikely background he managed to obtain a transfer to the Royal Flying Corps in 1917 but qualified as a pilot too late for hostilities. In early 1919 he was a flying instructor at the Royal Air Force station at Narborough and, realising that he stood little chance of being able to obtain a permanent commission in the newly established RAF, decided he had no choice but to pack his bags and take his chances with thousands of other ex-Service pilots. 'I had been told that some twenty-two thousand pilots would be returning to civilian life, and that there might be openings for one in a thousand of them. I was resolved to be such a one.'[1] Fortunately Alan Cobham was able to combine his flying skills with an ample helping of entrepreneurial flair.

He teamed up with brothers Fred and Jack Holmes to form Berkshire Aviation Tours Limited and approached the Aircraft Disposals Company at Waddon near Croydon where ex-RAF aircraft were being sold off cheaply. They started with one Avro504K priced at £450, one Ford car costing £200, petrol valued at £50 and a cash surplus of £200 – most of the money being borrowed.[2] Before long they had two Avro 504Ks, G-EAKX and G-EASF and between 1919 and 1921 travelled around the country using whatever rough fields they could find, selling joy-rides to the public and honing their flying skills at the same time. The economic slump of 1921 brought the near collapse of the company, by which time Cobham had moved on to the de Havilland Hire Company based at Stag Lane near the Edgware Road in north London, where he would undertake air photography and air taxi work.

One of the early contracts was with Aerofilms, the historic film archive, and when the weather was suitable flights in de Havilland DH9s were made throughout the country. One tour made over five days included Ipswich, Sandringham, Boston, Lincoln, York, Darlington, Newcastle and the Lake District, finishing in Bristol before heading back to Stag Lane. Other jobs included a stunt to distribute copies of the four o'clock edition of the *Star* newspaper to East Coast resorts at the same time as it was being read in London. On this occasion Cobham dropped newspapers off in Southend, Clacton, Lowestoft, Yarmouth and Norwich.

There was also air taxi work, for example in the autumn of 1921 delivering two former Royal Flying Corps DH9Cs to Seville in Spain, which had been bought from the Aircraft Disposals Company for the princely sum of £22 10s. before being serviced and repaired at Stag Lane. This venture introduced Cobham to the challenges of longer distance European flights which took in France, Morocco and Italy. In fact he became so well he became so well known that he was nicknamed 'le roi des taxi-pilots' ('the king of the taxi pilots'). The hire service began to expand and a number of new pilots joined, including Captain C. D. Barnard (see below) who would later make his name in long distance record flights and 'circus' flying.

As his career developed, so did his private life, for in 1922 he married the beautiful Gladys Lloyd, a celebrated actress, and for the best part of the next 50 years their partnership was a source of security and strength in Cobham's ambitions and schemes.

The Empire flights

Fresh possibilities emerged with a new aircraft, the DH50, a design which was developed from the ageing war surplus DH9. The aircraft had an enclosed cabin for four passengers (the pilot to the rear in an open cockpit) and utilised the DH9-type biplane wings, tail unit and part of the fuselage. Although it had a relatively short range and small payload the aircraft could operate out of any moderately sized field. The prototype G-EBFN first flew at Stag Lane in July 1923 and the following month Cobham took the machine to Gothenburg in Sweden for an International Aeronautical Conference where he won first prize in reliability trials. In the next three years Cobham was to make his name in the DH50, in long distance flights to Rangoon, Cape Town and to Melbourne in Australia.

The following year, 1924, Cobham entered the aircraft for the King's Cup, an all-round Britain air race organised on the principle of a motor rally, and won at a speed of 106 mph. By now he was attracting the attention of people in high places, not least the Secretary of State for Air Lord Thomson and the Director of Civil Aviation Air Vice-Marshal Sir Sefton Brancker, the men behind the ambitious Imperial Airship Programme to build the R100 and R101 as a means of flying over longer distances than any heavier-than-air machine could achieve, thus aiding communication within the scattered Empire territories.

Brancker persuaded Lord Thomson to finance a flight by Cobham to India to investigate the possibilities of using large hangars and mooring masts to handle the R101. Needless to say there was some haggling over the costs, with the Air Minister offering £750 maximum while de Havilland required a fee of £1,500. Eventually a compromise was found and Cobham, Brancker, with the engineer Arthur Elliot set off for India in November 1924, flying a second DH50 G-EBFO or 'Foxtrot Oscar'. After many adventures outside the scope of this book they reached Rangoon on 6 February. After Brancker had surveyed several sites they began the return journey on 28 February arriving back in Croydon on 17 March 1925 having flown 17,000 miles, 219 flying hours in 100 days, with 58 take-offs and landings, few of them on prepared aerodromes.

The success of the Rangoon trip convinced Cobham that flying had to be more than a mere 'stunt' over short distances and had the potential for long distance air transport, both for Imperial Airways and also for airship travel. He also relished the challenges of long endurance flights and the subsequent public adulation they generated. He even began to entertain the idea of an airline of his own.

He set his sights on Africa, most of which was under the British flag and obtained backing from Brancker, Sir Charles Wakefield of Castrol, the BP Company for fuel, and Imperial Airways for a pioneering flight to South Africa to explore the commercial possibilities of the route for air transport. Once again in G-EBFO, loaned to him by de Havilland, he set off on 15 November 1925 with Elliot as engineer and B. Emmott, film cameraman of Gaumonts, as there were prospects of lucrative film earnings. Cape

Town was reached on 17 February 1926 after a flight of 8,500 miles in 27 hops each of which had averaged 315 miles, over 93 days. The return journey began over the same route on 26 February and on 13 March Cobham landed back at Croydon only 15 days after setting off from Cape Town.

Many accolades followed, including an audience with King George V at Buckingham Palace who expressed great interest in the trip, the award of the Air Force Cross and the Royal Aero Club Gold Medal. Cobham had become an international celebrity.

Within days of returning from Cape Town he began to plan for his most ambitious adventure thus far. His imagination was stirred by the prospect of a flight to Australia, that most remote of Empire territories. Once again, the idea was to blaze the trail for an air service which it was felt would be best provided by the airship programme. With the backing of Wakefield, de Havilland, Armstrong Siddeley and the Air Ministry, Cobham made detailed preparations and set off from the River Medway at Rochester on 30 June 1926 for Melbourne accompanied by Elliot, this time with the DH50 on floats (wheels were sent by sea in advance so that the aircraft could be converted back for flying overland in Australia).

After an epic trip they arrived at Darwin after a flight lasting 37 days on 6 August. Then came the long overland leg to Sydney which was reached after another five days on 11 August – a total of 42 days from England to Sydney.

The homeward journey started on 27 August via Darwin, Singapore, India, Italy, and France, and on 1 October Cobham made a spectacular landing in the Thames in front of the Houses of Parliament, to a VIP reception including Lord Thomson, Brancker, Wakefield, the Speaker of the House of Commons, Members of both Houses and Geoffrey de Havilland. There was no doubting the scale of Cobham's achievement, 28,000 miles covered in 94 days – and this was fully recognised by the Government and the official functions in his honour which followed, culminating in the accolade of a Knighthood bestowed by King George V on 5 October.

What was left for this knight of the realm and celebrity to do? Cobham decided that he had sufficient influential contacts to resign from the de Havilland Company to set up on his own as Alan Cobham Aviation Limited and the following year went a step further and formed 'Cobham-Blackburn Air Lines Ltd' in partnership with an old friend Robert Blackburn. He began to think in terms of his original ambition of a round-the-world flight in the newly built Short Singapore flying boat, designed for RAF service and with a greater carrying capacity than the trusty DH50. However, this plan was one too far and he failed to obtain the necessary funds. Refusing to give up easily he produced a revised plan for a flight around Africa, partly to survey a possible route for Imperial Airways. Out of the total estimated costs of £20,000 he secured £12,000 from Sir Charles Wakefield, £3,000 from the Short Brothers, £1,000 from Rolls-Royce and the remainder from smaller donations.

The flight was named 'The Sir Charles Wakefield Flight of Survey round Africa' and Cobham and his crew of five including Lady Cobham set off on Thursday 17 November 1927 from Rochester. Many problems

'Airmindedness at Norwich'. Sir Alan Cobham's DH61 'Giant Moth'.
Sir Sefton Brancker alighting from the aircraft after a flight with Cobham. Less than a year later Brancker was killed in the R101 disaster. (Flightglobal Archive 23 May 1929 page 424)

were encountered, not least a two month delay in Malta due to weather damage to the aircraft with a further month in West Africa awaiting an engine change. The result was that Cobham did not arrive back at Plymouth until 31 May 1928, more than double the intended journey time. However, the trip was judged to be a success and another considerable achievement.

The 'Air Faring Outlook' and National Aviation Day

The success of the Empire flights gave Cobham the confidence to pursue his next ambition, the promotion of his passionate belief in air transport in every city, town and village in Britain. He made a start in purchasing the new DH61 'Giant Moth' G-AAEV at a cost of £3,250, an aircraft which had a wide cabin and space for up to ten passengers, the pilot in an open cockpit and a 450 hp Bristol Jupiter engine. He named the aircraft 'Youth of Britain' and began a 21 week propaganda tour of 110 towns and cities in Britain with a view to surveying possible municipal aerodrome sites. It was a mammoth effort in the course of which he gave short flights to 3,500 mayors and councillors and free flights to 10,000 children – all to further his concept of the 'Air Faring Outlook'. By October 1929 he had returned to Stag Lane and shortly afterwards delivered the DH61 to Imperial Airways in Salisbury, Rhodesia to which he had sold it for a price of £3,000. Sadly the aircraft was damaged in an accident shortly after it was passed on to its new owners, and written off.

October 1930 saw the demise of the hopes of an airship programme with the fatal crash of the R101 at Beauvais in France, resulting in 46 fatalities including Sir Sefton Brancker and Lord Thomson. In the meantime Cobham had reluctantly sold his fledgling Cobham-Blackburn Air Line and began to plan another African survey flight, this time in the three-motor, 16-passenger Short Valetta float seaplane. In July 1931 he set off with a five man crew, over the next 41 days covering 12,300 miles in 131 flying hours at an average speed of 94 mph.

By now his ambitions were of a more domestic nature in his plan for National Aviation Day tours with a fleet of aircraft, his appetite whetted by the reception of his 1929 venture. Once again, the aim was to promote 'air-mindedness' and he began to make detailed plans. First of all he required suitable aircraft and a competent team.

One of his first steps was to join the Board of the newly established Airspeed Ltd (see Chapter 7) under the management of two old friends A. H. Tiltman and Nevil Shute Norway, who had found themselves unemployed after the demise of the airship programme, although they had worked on the successful private R100 project. The aim of the firm was to manufacture light transport aircraft of the type that would suit Cobham's requirements. The upshot was the design and construction to his specifications of the Airspeed Ferry, a low cost, miniature, three-motor airliner capable of

BAE SYSTEMS

Airspeed Ferry G-ABSI delivered to Sir Alan Cobham April 1932.
(BAE SYSTEMS Photo ref: AS4-G2434)

carrying ten passengers in and out of small fields. Cobham ordered two in June 1931, just before he left on his African tour in the Valetta. The first Ferry G-ABSI was delivered in time for the start of his National Aviation Day tours on 24 April 1932 at a cost of £5,195. This was the start of what became known as 'Cobham's Flying Circus'.

Popular flying and the Norfolk scene

Norfolk was a favourite area for the early aviators, with its gentle undulating landscape, massive coastline and growing popular holiday seaside resorts like Hunstanton and Cromer, a tempting stage for young aviators eager to demonstrate their flying skills. This is what a young F. P. 'Freddie' Raynham had in mind when he flew to the area from Brooklands in July 1914 in his Avro 504 Waterplane, a machine sponsored for the planned *Daily Mail* Circuit of Britain Race. The spectacle at Hunstanton was watched by 12,000 people in near perfect weather before Raynham flew on to Cromer. The race had been scheduled for August but was abandoned by the declaration of war with Germany on 4 August.

Freddie Raynham and his Avro 504 Waterplane at Hunstanton, July 1914.
(RW from the Citizen, *16/4/1986)*

The war years left their mark on Norfolk with a legacy of numerous landing grounds and aerodromes but the post-war depression postponed any return to 'business as usual'. However during the 1920s there was a growing public appetite for the excitement that aerobatic displays could offer. A typical example was the 'crazy flying display' billed by a comparatively unknown airman called Captain Arthur Orde Bigg-Wither scheduled for King's Lynn on Sunday 2 May 1926. Bigg-Wither's background is fairly shadowy except that he was said to be 'well known' in London and lived in Waterloo Road, described as a poor neighbourhood. Little has come to light about his war record except that he was a pilot in the rank of second lieutenant serving in No. 40 Squadron Royal Flying Corps based in France in 1917. His wartime flying career appears to have been a short one, as he was listed as being severely injured in an accident in May 1917, just over a month after he had qualified as a pilot. Nevertheless he was granted a Short Service Commission in 1919 and was in the Reserve of Air Force Officers in 1924. It was claimed that he possessed 'private means' but after the war had drifted between commercial travelling and an attempt to start a hat-making business.

Bigg-Wither may have been a typical example of one of Cobham's twenty-two thousand ex-pilots looking for jobs at the end of the war, with openings for only one in a thousand of them. In any event Bigg-Wither put

Two images of Bigg-Wither's aircraft and crash in Hardwick Cemetery 2 May 1926.
Top: George Lloyd swings the propeller for start-up.
Below: Crash site in Hardwick. (Stan Langley)

to the test his aspirations as a display pilot and arranged for his machine, a Sopwith Gnu G-EAGP which was owned by the Lloyd Aviation Company, to be flown from Brooklands to Peterborough, dismantled and transported by train to King's Lynn, then reassembled and made ready for the display.

Stan Langley relates that the venue for the display was a field in the Exton's Road area owned by his uncle Charles Richmond who was a prominent Lynn businessman. After a test flight on the Saturday from a large field just over the Exton's Road earmarked as a landing ground, Bigg-

Another view of the crash in Hardwick Cemetery.

Present site of Bigg-Wither's unmarked grave

Wither began his display on the Sunday in front of about 2,000 spectators at Gaywood Hall and a few people were given pleasure flights. Later in the afternoon he took off again after a delay due to engine trouble, accompanied by a local man Arthur Golding Barrett and stunt wing walker George Mark Lloyd, who was the aircraft's owner. A gale was blowing but the stunt man performed his wing walking as planned but in the course of some aerobatics disaster struck, the engine stopped and the aircraft spiralled out of control and crashed in the old part of Hardwick Cemetery. Bigg-Wither was killed, Lloyd was seriously injured and Barrett escaped with minor injuries – all of this in the presence of a Miss Rosa Wilson, Bigg-Wither's fiancée.

It is sad to relate that Bigg-Wither is buried in Hardwick Cemetery, only 20 yards from his crash site in an unmarked grave. Presumably his comparative lack of means and absence of immediate family (his next of kin were domiciled in Burma) could explain this solitary and anonymous fate.

In October 1929, another freelance aviator Captain Earl Bateman 'Batty' Fielden hired a field at North Lynn Farm, Estuary Road, King's Lynn, to give aerobatic displays of stunt flying and five shilling joy-rides in his Avro 504, with the added bonus that the first-ever aerial photographs were taken of the town by an airsick *Lynn News* photographer. As the display was scheduled over a weekend Fielden had promised that there would be no flying during Divine Services! With a distinguished war record behind him, he had been an instructor at the Yorkshire Aeroplane Club since 1926

First ever aerial view of King's Lynn taken by Capt. E. B. Fielden, October 1929. Of interest are the lack of cars and the faded patch in the middle of the market place which marked the site of the ornamental drinking fountain and gas lamp which had been demolished in 1926. (RW from the Citizen, *23/11/1988)*

and in 1930 founded Aviation Tours Ltd, becoming managing director and chief test pilot.

In February 1927 the Norfolk and Norwich Aero Club had been established at Mousehold Heath in Norwich, later a centre during the war years for aeroplane production and testing. The site was earmarked as the new Norwich airport which was officially opened by the Prince of Wales in 1933.

Heacham and Hunstanton were rapidly growing Norfolk seaside resorts, ideal for the sort of display flying that was becoming popular by the later 1920s. In the summer of 1928 the Berkshire Aviation Company had laid on a display by an Avro 504 three-seater at Heacham South Beach, also offering joy rides to passengers.

In July 1931 the distinguished airman Captain C. D. Barnard arrived at Heacham with what was claimed to be 'The World's First Air Circus'. The venue was a large field known as Stoney Hills, behind Church Farm where a small civil landing ground had become established.[3] Charles Douglas Barnard was another pioneering airman who, like Cobham, might have stepped from the pages of *The Boy's Own Paper*. In fact his exploits were recounted in *The Modern Boy* of September 1930 under the heading 'Adventures in the Air'. He had served in the Royal Flying Corps before becoming a test pilot with the Sopwith Aviation Company and from 1920-27 with the de Havilland Aviation Company. He was credited with a number of record-breaking flights including the first London to Malta flight in 1923, and as the personal pilot to Mary, Duchess of Bedford, 'the flying Duchess', a number of long endurance flights including one to Europe and North Africa in 1927. Then, accompanied by the Duchess as his sponsor, he undertook a record-breaking flight to Karachi and back, in a previously unlucky Fokker 12-seater monoplane called 'The Spider' which now had a new lease of life with its Bristol Jupiter engine. The trip totalling 10,000 miles took 88½ flying hours over 7½ days by a series of short 'hops'. For this achievement he was awarded the Royal Aero Club Gold Medal. The following year they flew to Cape Town and back, covering 19,000 miles in 20 days. The serious purpose behind these flights was to chart the commercial possibilities of flights to these regions and to provide better communications within the scattered Empire territories.

The 'Spider' had pride of place in the display but Barnard's 'circus' also included an unusual Cierva autogyro, which anticipated the modern helicopter design, and five other aircraft. Admission to the display was one shilling for adults, sixpence for children, and flights were charged at five shillings. The various antics included aerobatics, a parachute descent, wing-walking and bombing a car with flour.

The success of the display led to Sir Alan Cobham choosing the field for his displays which soon followed.

Cobham's Flying Circus in Norfolk – 'Let's go up and fly'

By the spring of 1932 Cobham was ready to begin his National Aviation Day tours, for which his aircraft collection included the two Airspeed Ferries G-ABSI (*Youth of Britain II*) and G-ABSJ (*Youth of Britain III*), a Handley Page W.10 G-EBMR chartered from Imperial Airways nicknamed 'The Giant Airliner', a Tiger Moth G-ABUL, four Avro 504s, a Cierva autogyro G-ABGB, a Southern Martlet G-ABBN, a DH60G Moth G-ABJC and a two-seat glider BAC VII. His team included Captain Percival Phillips, a skilled and experienced pilot. The first venue was at Hanworth Air Park on 12 April and the team worked throughout the next few months, arriving at Peterborough on Tuesday 19 July and Stoney Hills in Heacham on the 20th.

It was a day to remember, with ten aeroplanes carrying out the usual mix of pleasure flights, aerobatics, a parachute drop, wing-walking and 'crazy flying'. The *Lynn Advertiser* described Sir Alan as 'a short, keen-looking man, a little under forty years of age' with unbounded enthusiasm

Airspeed Ferry and the National Aviation Day display.

for his aim to influence local authorities in the need for landing grounds – 'What is Lynn doing about it?' – being his first question to a reporter.

There was one unscripted event during the afternoon when Cobham flew to Skegness with a local man Mr R. Dunseath, an accountant, to check on the progress of the Handley Page airliner being repaired after damage on landing to its port wing and undercarriage. All was well at Skegness but as Cobham started the engine for the return journey the aircraft bounded forward and spun, nearly hitting Dunseath, before damaging the propeller of the Handley Page. Eventually a new propeller was sent for and both machines returned with no more problems.

Official Programme of Cobham's National Aviation Day Display.

Arrival of Cobham's Flying Circus at Heacham.
Left to right: two Desoutters, DH60 Moth, Airspeed Ferry,
DH Tiger Moth, Avro 504K.

The day was described as an outstanding success, but there was no let up as the team moved on to Thetford on the 21st, Cromer on the 22nd, Norwich on the 23rd , Yarmouth on the 24th followed by Ipswich, Clacton and further down the coast towards various locations in Kent. By the end of the season a total of 187 towns and cities had been visited.

Memories of Cobham's visits to the Stoney Hills field at Heacham are still fresh. Dick Garwood of Heacham recalled being mad on aeroplanes

Another view of the Circus – Avro 504K in foreground.

Martin Hearn, one of Cobham's daring young men, giving a display at Heacham.

NATIONAL AVIATION DAY CRUSADE

SIR ALAN COBHAM'S
GREAT
AIR DISPLAY

20 Spectacular Events - Twice Daily
Including—

Demonstration of advanced aerobatics and upside-down flying.
Thrilling Parachute Descents.
Wireless-controlled flying and aeroplanes dancing in the air to music.
Miniature Schneider Trophy Race.
Daring delayed-drop parachute descent.
Demonstrations of the Autogiro.
Aerobatic thrills for passengers.
Smoke Stunting—The pilot's evolutions traced by smoke.
Thrilling exhibitions of wing-walking and trapeze acrobatics in the air.
An opportunity for a war-time pilot.
Humorous and surprise items, "The Battle of the Flours" and "Aerial
    Pig-sticking."
Speed and height judging competitions.
Grand Fly-past and Parade of Aircraft.

Cruises in Air Liners. Flying Lessons
Short Flights in the "Moth" and other
open aeroplanes. Autogiro Flights.
Passengers carried in many display events.

Church Farm, Aylmerton
CROMER
FOR ONE DAY ONLY !
THURSDAY, AUGUST 17th, 1933
Two Complete Displays 2-15 and 7 p.m.
Admission 1/3 Children 6d. Cars 1/-
Flights from 4/-.

"MAKE THE SKYWAYS BRITAIN'S HIGHWAYS"

Poster advertising Cobham's Flying Circus at Cromer, 17 August 1933.

at the age of eight and spending all his days at Stoney Hills during 'Circus' visits. He managed to persuade his father to pay for a trip in one of the aircraft which had 'wicker baskets fixed to the floor and the tip of each lower wing on which a parachutist would stand. When they pulled the rip cord the slipstream would pull them off. The trip took us round the coast to Brancaster and back to Heacham. My aunt aged about 26 at the time volunteered to fly in a two seat aircraft to do aerobatics and cut paper streamers with the aircraft propellers.' Another event recalled was for one of the aeroplanes to fly off and drop a rugby ball, which if retrieved and brought back earned the finder a free flight.

Wing Commander Ken Wallis recalled the many air shows being held in the eastern counties at the time, not all of them Cobham's. Many of the antics employed would today be regarded as 'hairy' to say the least, for example some of the wing-walking demonstrations. Also it was not unusual to experience the 'loop' without being formally strapped in, the pilot having to ensure the maintenance of positive 'g'!

For the 1933 season Cobham operated two separate tours from April to September. The No. 1 tour gave over 100 displays in 137 days throughout Britain and Southern Ireland. No. 2 tour team visited Cromer on 16 and 17 August followed by Lowestoft, Norwich and Yarmouth. Then it was the turn of Peterborough on 22 September, East Dereham on the 23rd and Hunstanton on the 24th. The venue on that day was stated to have been Courtyard Farm, Ringstead, and nine aircraft took part including the Airspeed Ferry, and a collection of Moth aircraft – DH Moth, Tiger Moth, Fox Moth, together with a Cierva C10 autogyro, the ubiquitous Avro 504 and Avro 640 Club Cadet. The display programme offered parachute descents, smoke stunting, aerobatics, inverted flying, crazy flying and paper cutting. Joy-rides continued until dusk and the following day the circus left for North Walsham.

There was a return to the Courtyard Farm field during the 1934 season on Saturday 1 September during the Norfolk tour which had included Yarmouth on 30 August and Cromer on the 31st. The Ringstead event was marred by a heavy thunderstorm later in the afternoon but there were a few new and exciting features including a high speed run by Flight Lieutenant Geoffrey Tyson at nearly 300 mph flying a Armstrong-Siddeley engined Blackburn 'Lincock', a glider display by Joan Meakin and a parachute descent by Ivor Price.

John Coady was an 13-year old living at Stoke Ferry and he related how Sir Alan Cobham was offering flights from a field on the Whittington

BRITISH HOSPITALS' GREAT
AIR PAGEANT

Led by

Chas. W. A. SCOTT, A.F.C.
England-Australia Record Holder.

Pilots Include

Hon. Mrs. VICTOR BRUCE

MISS PAULINE GOWER and

MISS DOROTHY SPICER

PROGRAMME INCLUDES :-
Great Air Race.   Grand Formation Flight.   Wireless Controlled Flying. Spectacular Aerobatic Flying.   Crazy Flying. Humorous Events. Aerial Marksmanship. Wing Walking Demonstration. Surprise Items. Thrilling Parachute Descents. «Daily Sketch» Flying Lesson,   etc., etc.

PASSENGER FLIGHTS
Fly in the actual Aeroplane in which Mr. SCOTT made his Record Flights to and from Australia. Passenger flights in the new Air Liner " The D.H. Dragon."   Aerobatic Flights. Formation Flights.   Flying Lessons.   Air Taxi Flights. Flights at 200 m.p.h.

PASSENGER FLIGHTS FROM 4/-
Free Flight Competitions

MORRIS TRANSPORT THROUGHOUT.
COME TO THE PAGEANT & HELP *YOUR* HOSPITAL.

FREE FLIGHT TICKETS
will be presented to Patrons of the
MAJESTIC
at evening performances on July 31st & Aug. 1st during the Showing of " THE BLONDE CAPTIVE " Retain your half Cinema Ticket

---

Printed by Galbraith King & Co., Ltd., 44, Fenchurch Street, London, E.C.3.

Poster advertising British Hospitals' Air Pageant in King's Lynn, 2 August 1933.

side of the River Wissey, probably during the 1934 season. He paid five shillings for a flight in a 'biplane' with three seats, the pilot, himself and a young couple. 'We flew around the Stoke Ferry area for about 15 minutes. It was wonderful for me as one seldom saw any aeroplanes at all at that time. My mother had kittens when I got home and told her.' He went on to join the RAF in 1938 and served at Bircham Newton. He left the Service in 1947 but continued to fly with the Norfolk and Norwich Aero Club at Swanton Morley.

Not all of Cobham's customers were totally satisfied, as testified by Anthony Maynard when he recalled the experience of his parents during their courting days at Croydon: 'Billboards at the show were offering flights for, I think, half a crown, which was not insubstantial to an impecunious young bachelor. Regarding it perhaps as an investment, courtshipwise, my father indulged the two of them, but was extremely mortified when the advertised flight turned out to be no more than taking off, going round and landing. Pa apparently got a bit verbal with Cobham, who was milking the adoration and the clicking of Brownie Boxes, and was arrogantly given short shrift!'

What appears to have been Cobham's final visit with his team was on Monday 29 July 1935, when he returned to the Stoney Hills field with what was claimed to be a number of new features, including high speed aerobatics by a Comper Swift G-ABPY, the Cierva G-ACYH and Flight Lieutenant Tyson putting Tiger Moth G-ACEZ through its paces with inverted flying, picking up the handkerchief and looping the loop. There was also a parachute jump by Miss Naomi Heron-Maxwell, a well-known female parachutist. The admission to the display was one shilling three pence for adults and one shilling was charged for cars.

By 1936 Cobham's interests were developing in the direction of air-to-air refuelling in which he was to break revolutionary new ground, and C. W. A. Scott (see below) and Percival Phillips joined forces to buy the National Aviation Day operation under a new company called C. W. A. Scott's Flying Display Ltd with *Flying for All* as its theme.

The 1930s saw display flying coming into its own, long before the advent of stringent safety rules, high fuel costs and insurance charges. It was Sir Alan Cobham who dominated the scene and led the way for the many others who followed. Frivolity and fun played its part (often in short supply at the time) but so did flying skill, daring, detailed planning and organisation, in which Cobham excelled. Pleasure flights usually cost anything from half a crown to five shillings and were eagerly saved up for by budding aviators – five shillings in the early 1930s could for example equate with half the weekly council rent for a three-roomed house in Sheffield.[4] There is ample evidence that Cobham's public displays influenced a whole generation of youngsters who might otherwise have given little thought to aeroplanes and aviation. Neville Duke, later the RAF's highest-scoring fighter pilot and supersonic test pilot, recalled saving his pocket money for joy-riding flights with Cobham's Circus. Dizzy Addicot, later a display pilot himself and Vickers-Armstrong test pilot from 1955-1979 related that at the age of ten he sat on his father's knee in an Avro 504 being flown by Cobham at Weston-super-Mare and 'I was hooked from then on'. Wing Commander Les Harland, whose air experience spanned flying bombers in the Desert Air Force at Alamein to helicopters during the 1950s Malayan emergency recalled being given five shillings by his grandmother to pay for a flight with the Flying Circus at Knavesmire near York. Jimmy Dell, later test pilot on the Lightning and TSR2, had his imagination fired when Cobham's Circus visited Liverpool. It was claimed that almost 75 per cent of applicants for the Royal Air Force at the start of the war had first learned about aeroplanes and flying through Cobham and his Flying Circus. Nevil Shute's novel *Round the Bend* published in 1951, features a young man who joins the Circus for casual work as it moves around the country, and later takes up flying as a career. There must been few locations throughout Britain and Ireland where people had not heard of Sir Alan Cobham's Flying Circus.

Cobham's wider vision of 'municipal aerodromes' throughout the country never truly came to fruition with his notion of small-scale localised air travel within reach of the majority of the population. It is open to question what he would have made of today's air transport, concentrated in a few massive centres which have become something of a nightmare to the tens of thousands of air travellers who have to use them.

The British Hospitals Air Pageant and Pauline Gower

During the early 1930s the air display scene was getting crowded, with scores of different individuals and teams competing throughout the summer seasons, including the British Hospitals Air Pageant (BHAP) in 1933, led by C. W. A. Scott AFC, who in the previous year had broken the England-to-Australia record in eight days, 20 hours and 42 minutes over the 10,000 mile distance. Charles Scott was another of those larger than life personalities who dominated the world of aviation between the wars. A

Londoner, he had obtained a Short Service Commission in the RAF and learned to fly at Duxford, where a fellow cadet was the Scotsman Jim Mollison, later to be another aviation record-holder and future husband of Amy Johnson. After an unspectacular period in the RAF Scott left to become an airline pilot in Australia but soon quarrelled with his employers and took up flying in a freelance capacity. He combined the skills of a brilliant flyer with the unlikely attributes of a heavyweight boxing champion, a classical pianist and a poet. An observer during his time in Australia recalled that 'Scott might have been good at Beethoven but he could also knock over an 18-stone shearer without even putting his glass down'.[5]

The Hospitals' Pageant included amongst others, the up-and-coming aviator Pauline Gower with her mechanic Dorothy Spicer and in the six months from April to October 185 towns were visited with over 8,000 passengers carried. Life was tough for the circus flyers with pilots and mechanics having to sleep in tents for a night or two before moving on to

Sky Devils Air Circus Programme leaflet, Gorleston 1934.

another location. Norfolk was reached in early August 1933 when the Pageant moved from Felixstowe to Thetford on the 1st, then to King's Lynn and a field behind Gaywood Hall on the 2nd and 3rd, with Spalding next on the list. The Pageant was not an outstanding success, the £6,800 sum raised for the local hospitals falling well short of the target of £20,000. The following year saw the BHAP rebranded as 'The Sky Devils Air Circus' but the tour was not a success due to competition from Cobham's Circus and smaller operators.

It may have been the brief visit to Norfolk in 1933, or the desire to settle in one place for a while that persuaded Pauline Gower and Dorothy Spicer to set up an air taxi and pleasure flight business in Hunstanton during the summers of 1933 and 1934. The Searle family, who were in the catering and tourist business, rented out some land to the girls, now the site of the Searle's caravan park, and they lived in a gypsy caravan with their two dogs close to their blue Spartan three-seater aircraft named 'Helen of Troy'. Air taxi trips were offered from Hunstanton to Skegness, joy rides at three shillings and sixpence for 1½ minutes and five shillings for a flight around the town, sometimes with the added bonus of being able to 'bomb' Mr Searle's speedboat with bags of flour. A return flight to Skegness would cost one pound. On a bank holiday providing the weather was suitable around 150 passengers could be carried, bringing in takings of around £30. Crazy flying displays were laid on and in due course parachute descents by Bill Williams who had joined their team. In early 1934 Pauline Gower and her partners created a company called Air Trips Ltd to put the venture on more of a sound footing and business boomed with Pauline claiming a world record for women pilots, having organised 10,000 passenger flights without mishap.

For the 1935 season Pauline invested in a DH83 Fox Moth now registered G-ADNF. A setback occurred on one of the early trips with two passengers when the engine failed and the machine crash-landed into a swamp, fortunately without serious injury to anyone on board. The local press had a field day with one headline proclaiming 'Miss Gower's Skill prevents Disaster'. Luckily Pauline still had the faithful Spartan and business could resume, with the 1935 season ending on an upbeat note.

Aviation was one of the few activities in the 1930s which could offer women some independence from the stuffy social conventions of the day and a few like Pauline Gower seized the opportunity. Possessing private means was clearly an advantage but even someone from a fairly modest background like Amy Johnson could take up the challenge with the right blend of enthusiasm, aptitude and being in the right place at the right time. This opened the door to a whole generation of women who became pilots in the Air Transport Auxiliary (ATA) during the war, delivering aircraft from the factories to the airfields. Pauline Gower went on to be a successful ATA pilot and married Wing Commander Bill Fahie in June 1945. Sadly she died in childbirth on 3 March 1947 at the age of 35. Her former mechanic Dorothy Spicer was killed the previous year with her husband on board an Avro York which crashed into mountains in Brazil, with the loss of all passengers and crew.[6]

The era of the freelance flyers and flying circuses was gradually drawing to a close by the later 1930s. Royal Air Force stations began to host what became known as Empire Air Days and the more serious side of aviation asserted itself with the RAF expansion programme. A typical example was Bircham Newton's first Empire Air Day at the end of May 1935. An estimated 6,000 spectators watched aerobatics, formation flying and inspected ground displays of aircraft and the work of the station. The *Lynn Advertiser* of 31 May made special mention of the aerial photography work which 'had been of great assistance in determining the existence of ancient settlement sites and trackways.' Examples quoted were at Brancaster, March and Colchester. However, the threat from the rise of Hitler and a rearmed Germany produced, as Cobham himself admitted 'the real boost in aviation development' but Cobham and others played a major part in an important era of aviation in which people were able to enjoy flying for its own sake.

Notes:
[1] Sir Alan Cobham, *A Time to Fly* pp 31-32.
[2] For cost and price comparisons see 'A Note on Money and Buying Power'.
[3] Grid ref TF697384.
[4] The cost of a flight offered by Classic Wings over Norwich in a vintage eight-seater Dragon Rapide in May 2010 was £79 per person.
[5] Quoted in *Mollison: The Flying Scotsman* by P. Luff p101.
[6] 8 March 2010 was the centenary of the first woman in the world to achieve a pilot's licence, Élise Deroche, at Châlons in France. The first British woman to do so was Mrs Hilda Hewlett at Brooklands on 29 August 1911.

9

Lawrence Edwards –
The First Officer Prisoner of War

A young New Zealander named Lawrence 'Laurie' Hugh Edwards, a pilot in No. 206 Squadron based at Bircham Newton in Norfolk, had the dubious distinction of becoming the first New Zealander and the first Allied officer of any of the armed services, to become a prisoner of war in Germany.

Born in June 1913 of English parents, the young 'Laurie' was brought up in Patea in Taranaki, North Island. He showed little academic prowess at school but achieved distinction as an all-round sportsman especially in rugby, cricket and surf life-saving. Enlisting as a private in the Territorial Army in 1933, he moved to Wellington in 1935 and was employed as a stock clerk in a meat exporting company. His main claim to fame during this period was as an outstanding rugby player and a brilliant wing three-quarter, first in Taranaki from 1933. Taking part in trials for the All Blacks in two successive years, he was considered unlucky not be selected for his country. However in one season he played for 'The Rest' against the All Blacks and from 1935 for North Island and also Wellington.

Laurie enrolled as a civilian pilot trainee for elementary flying training at Wellington Aero Club from 20 June until 12 September 1938 and then proceeded to the Royal New Zealand Air Force Flying Training School at Wigram, Christchurch (the first military airfield in New Zealand). Commissioned as Acting Pilot Officer in RNZAF, he was granted his flying badge on 31 January 1939 and qualified as a pilot in March 1939, having amassed a total of 138 hours' flying experience with a reputation as 'a steady and reliable pilot'.

Like thousands of his fellow countrymen he wasted no time in heeding the call to rally to the defence of the mother country and on 17 April 1939 left New Zealand for England in SS *Waimarama* in the company of several other young New Zealanders. Granted a short-service commission in the Royal Air Force on 20 May 1939 for a period of five years, he was posted to No. 206 Squadron at Bircham Newton in Norfolk which was equipped with the Avro Anson Mark I, at that time the backbone of RAF Coastal Command.

War and Capture

It was only a matter of a few months before war with Germany was declared on 3 September 1939, and immediately the squadron began offensive patrolling in the North Sea, especially on the look-out for U-Boats and enemy surface ships. The following day, 4 September, Bomber Command carried out the first offensive operation of the war from Wattisham in Suffolk when a mixed formation of Wellingtons and Blenheims took off to attack German ships off Wilhelmshaven and Brunsbüttel in the mouth of the Kiel Canal. Five Blenheims and two Wellingtons were shot down, the first RAF casualties of the war, and the first British prisoners taken, all being other ranks.

Pilot Officer Lawrence Edwards had already carried out his first coastal patrol which proved uneventful and on the third day of the war, 5 September, he took off in Anson I K6183 VX-B (VX being the wartime code of 206 Squadron) on his second (and final) operation with crew Sergeant Alexander Heslop, Leading Aircraftman (LAC) John Quilter and Aircraftman First Class (AC1) Geoffrey Sheffield. Their task was to carry out an anti-submarine patrol off Heligoland but the Anson was attacked by a marauding Heinkel He 115 seaplane of the Luftwaffe unit I/KuFlGr 160. In this unequal contest the crew of the underpowered and lightly armed Anson fought back, hindered by a series of gun-stoppages, until the aircraft was riddled with bullets and caught fire, eventually crash-landing in the sea somewhere near Dogger Bank and disintegrating. Edwards, badly injured and suffering severe burns, managed to struggle to the surface in his Mae West, helped by his ability as a strong swimmer, but the remainder of his crew were lost and no trace of them was ever found.[1] One report claimed that a German U-Boat surfaced to pick up Edwards, but he later stated that the German pilot, keen for confirmation of his 'kill', landed on the sea near the wrecked aircraft and took him on board. From there Edwards was flown to the island of Norderney, one of the East Frisian islands, for emergency treatment[2], and thence to hospital in Wesermünde near Hanover where he met up with Aircraftman L. G. Slattery (who had a broken jaw) and Sergeant Observer G. F. Booth (who had a broken foot), both from No. 107 Squadron and shot down in the first Bomber Command raid of 4 September and the first British (other rank) prisoners of war.

Back at Bircham Newton this first loss on operations was keenly felt. Ernest Fitchew, then a Sergeant-pilot with 206 Squadron (later Squadron

Place.	Date.	Time.	Summary of Events.	to Appendices.
			Sergeants' Mess and Quarters, N.A.A.F.I. and Sick Quarters. Additional hangar space is being provided by the erection of 3 Bellman hangars. The Operations Room, a wooden hut protected by sandbags, is manned in 6 hour periods by 3 watches, each consisting of a Controller, Navigation Officer, Cypher Officer and Plotting Officer.	
		1350	Three aircraft of 206 (G.R.) Squadron engaged on parallel track search for enemy submarines in area bounded by parallels 52°30′N. and 53°30′N., meridian 002°E. and Dutch territorial waters. All aircraft returned, no enemy having been sighted.	
	5/9	0515	Twelve aircraft of 206 (G.R.) Squadron engaged on parallel track search from a datum line 54°00′N. 0°23′E. to 52°02′N. 1°50′E. to a depth of 150 miles or as far as territorial waters. One aircraft had W/T failure and returned to base. Aircraft K 6187, B/206, pilot P/o BARNITT, navigator P/o KEEN, crew L.A.C. THOMPSON, sighted and attacked a hostile submarine at 0817 hrs. in position 53°10′N. 3°45′E. ('about 85 miles N.E. of LOWESTOFT). One 100lbs. A/S bomb was dropped and seen to explode within 50 ft. of the submarine when it was just submerged. After circling round another bomb was dropped on the estimated position of the submarine. Damage unknown.	
			One aircraft, K 6185, B/206, pilot P/o EDWARDS, navigator Sgt.HESLOP, crew L.A.C. QUILTER and A.C. SHEFFIELD, did not return and is presumed lost.	
			NOTE:- Two or three days subsequent to this German broadcasts stated that a British aircraft had been shot down over the NORTH SEA and that P/o L.H.EDWARDS, a NEW ZEALANDER, had been picked up by a German flying boat and was now in hospital at BREMEN.	

No. 206 Squadron Operations Record Book extract, 5 September 1939, reporting the loss of Pilot Officer Edwards and crew.

REPORTED MISSING

PILOT-OFFICER L. H. EDWARDS

WELL-KNOWN RUGBY PLAYER

Cabled advice that Pilot-Officer Laurence Hugh Edwards, of the Royal Air Force, and a former well-known Wellington Rugby player, has been "reported missing on patrol," has been received from the Air Ministry, London, by his parents, Mr. and Mrs. C. A. Edwards, of Patea. Pilot-Officer Edwards was formerly employed by Messrs. W. R. Fletcher, Ltd., of Wellington and Patea, and had been for some time in the Wellington office until he entered the New Zealand Royal Air Force in July last year. He commenced his training in New Zealand at Wellington on June 20 last year, and was transferred to Wigram on September 2, 1938. He reported for duty with the Royal Air Force, England, on May 19 last.

The patrol duties referred to are believed to be those which involved British casualties during the attack on the German fleet at Wilhelmshaven.

Well known on the Rugby field, Pilot-Officer Edwards was a brilliant wing-three-quarter. He represented Taranaki and later Wellington, and also played in the North Island team. His last game for Wellington was played in Christchurch last year after he had begun Air Force training. He left Wellington shortly before the Wellington team went on tour; but received special leave to play for the team against Southland and also against Canterbury.

FIRST CANADIAN CASUALTY

(Received September 7, 2.20 p.m.)

VICTORIA (B.C.), September 6. Anthony Playfair, aged 25, a pilot officer in the R.A.F., is the first Canadian war casualty. The War Ministry has informed his parents that he died on active service.

Pilot-Officer L. H. Edwards.

New Zealand newspaper report of 7 September 1939 of Plt Off. Edwards' loss.

this was a New Zealand sensation!

NZ PILOT WAS...
PIONEER PRISONER
OF WORLD WAR II

Within three days of the Allies' declaration of war on Germany, following Hitler's invasion of Poland in September 1939, a New Zealand airman fell into the hands of the enemy and was the first British officer and the first New Zealander to become a prisoner of war in World War Two.

The man taken prisoner was Pilot Officer Laurence Hugh Edwards (now Wing Commander Edwards, Commanding Officer of the R.N.Z.A.F. Officers' School, Whenuapai). He was flying with the R.A.F. as a Coastal Command pilot when war broke out.

Son of a well-known Patea family, Edwards was an outstanding all-round athlete and was especially good at rugby. He was chosen to play for Taranaki in his first year as a senior player and was in his day one of the finest wing three-quarters in the country. On two occasions he played for the North Island and was considered most unlucky to miss All Black honours. He did play against the All Blacks, however, in a Rest of New Zealand side.

Transferring to Wellington from Taranaki in 1936, Edwards undertook a short service commission in the Air Force, and in April, 1939, he left to undergo a course of instruction with the R.A.F. in England. He was a good pilot and had qualified for his wings before leaving New Zealand.

Posted to No. 48 Squadron, which was equipped with Ansons, Edwards became the seventh New Zealand pilot to be placed on strength. This squadron had always had a close association with New Zealanders. In 1918, as a fighter reconnaissance unit, it had been commanded by Sir Keith Park

Crown Studio.

Before he left New Zealand to join the R.A.F. L. H. Edwards was an outstanding rugby footballer, having twice played for the North Island against the South and also for a New Zealand XV against the All Blacks. Picture was taken at that time.

mitter and we are sure they would like to know how you are being treated.

P/O Edwards: I am being treated very well indeed. I am being treated like a German officer.

Announcer: I hope you are feeling well. We shall do anything for you that we can. We want you to feel that you are not wasting the years that you wanted to spend in New Zealand in civilian flying.

Number Six

The broadcast did not give an indication of the date or the place of the crash, nor of the prisoners' place of detention.

It was learned later, however, that the crash had taken place somewhere near Dogger Bank and that Edwards was interned in a Luftwaffe prison camp on the Island of Norderney.

The following month, in October, further advice was received through the Interna-

Article from 'Freedom', December 1955.

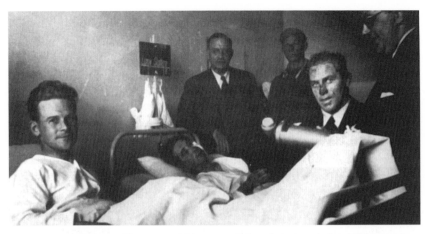

George Booth, Larry Slattery and Lawrence Edwards in hospital at Wesermünde,
being interviewed by German and American journalists, September 1939. Edwards
on right shows signs of burn injuries on his face. (Charles Rollings)

Leader) and newly returned from secondment to Bomber Command,
recalled the occasion:

'On my return to Bircham Newton I was informed of the loss of
"Jumbo" and his crew [the nickname presumably reflecting Edwards'
athletic prowess], who were shot down soon after the declaration of war.
Being a good swimmer Jumbo was able to survive the ditching. I always
say that 206 Squadron had the first POW!'

In this early period of the war, termed the 'Phoney War' or 'Sitzkrieg',
prisoners of war (later called 'kriegies') were something of a novelty on
both sides – until the spring of 1940 the total of RAF and Dominion Air
Force prisoners held in Germany remained under 40, compared to 13,022
by 1945. However during September 1939 there were 700,000 Polish
prisoners in German hands to be accommodated, which had a considerable
effect on available prisoner facilities. From what Edwards had learned about
the Nazis in Germany he expected a rough reception but was pleasantly
surprised that not only was he well treated by his captors but Luftwaffe
aircrew visited him in the evenings to chat about topics that would have
been familiar in any RAF mess. He was struck by their apparent lack of
interest in Hitler or Göring, but by their strong belief in the strength of the
German cause. Slattery and Booth, as the first two prisoners of war, were
even transported to Berlin for a 'friendly' interview with Reichmarshal
Hermann Göring himself.

At home, the fate of Lawrence Edwards was unknown for several days. Then *The Times* newspaper of 16 September reported a 'broadcast' from Zeesen in Germany, of an interview claiming to be with three captured RAF airman, Pilot Officer Edwards, Aircraftman Slattery and Sergeant Observer Booth – it was wrongly assumed that they were all from the same crash. The broadcast was heard by short-wave listeners in various parts of the world and Edwards' voice came over in tired and spiritless tones describing the moment he found himself in the water and the German pilot who shot him down had landed, threw him a rope and took him aboard the aircraft. It was suggested that the airmen did not realise that their conversations were being broadcast (although the transcript appears to contradict this) but in any case nothing of any substance was revealed:

Announcer: 'How are you feeling now? It must mean a great deal to you to be reduced to inactivity so early in the war. How are you going to employ your time?'

Edwards: 'I intend to learn the German language if I can. I hope it is possible to get some books from England so that I can continue my studies.'

Announcer: 'This is a question we would like to have your answer to because it is a question which will interest listeners abroad, particularly in New Zealand. This recording will be transmitted to New Zealand by the beam transmitter and we are sure they would like to know how you are being treated.'

Edwards: 'I am being treated very well indeed. I am being treated like a German officer.'

Announcer: 'I hope you are feeling well. We shall do anything for you that we can. We want you to feel that you are not wasting the years that you wanted to spend in New Zealand in civilian flying.'[3]

The broadcast did not contain any indication of the date or place of the crash, nor of where the prisoners were being held. The outcome of the broadcast was however significant as it was the first indication that Edwards was a POW, although at this stage he was still posted as 'missing' in the absence of official confirmation of his capture. A letter was sent to his father Mr C. A. Edwards in Patea outlining the news thus far and the local press in early September reported the loss of a 'well-known rugby player'.

Slattery and Edwards at Oflag IX A/H, Spangenberg Castle. (Charles Rollings)

Prisoner of War Camp

At the end of September Lawrence Edwards, termed Prisoner of War No. 6, was sent to Itzehöe (Oflag – Officers' Camp - XA), a Polish prisoners' camp about 30 miles east of Hamburg where about 600 Polish officers and soldiers were interned. There was little provision here for the few RAF and Fleet Air Arm prisoners and on 16 October Edwards and his fellow prisoners were transferred to Oflag IX A/H in Spangenberg Castle, a grim and impregnable fortress south of Kassel. This was a formidable medieval castle which had been used as a POW camp during the Franco-Prussian War, and then converted for use as a forestry school until its reopening as a POW camp for British and French Air Force officers. In spite of harsh surroundings the prisoners at first fared reasonably well. It was only as the war progressed and the numbers multiplied that the privations worsened. By the end of October 1939, official confirmation of Edwards as a prisoner had still not been received but a personal letter had been sent by him to a friend in England stating that he was out of hospital and now interned in a prison camp in Germany.

Edwards was soon joined by other RAF prisoners, including Wing Commander Harry 'Wings' Day, who was later to achieve fame as a survivor of the 'Great Escape' from Stalag Luft III. Other notables who arrived in due course included Anthony Barber, later Chancellor of the Exchequer, Aidan Crawley and fighter ace Robert Stanford-Tuck. Needless to say the German claim that Spangenberg was escape-proof offered little more than a challenge to the inmates but in spite of many daring and ingenious attempts no successful 'home-runs' were achieved by any escapers throughout Spangenberg's period as a camp.

The mood darkened in early 1941 when the German authorities received rumours of alleged ill-treatment of German POWs at Fort Henry in Canada, reports which later proved to be false. In reprisal, in March the Air Force prisoners at Spangenberg were moved out and transferred to Fort XV at Thorn in Poland, 100 miles north-west of Warsaw, a 'Straflager' or punishment camp, one of five forts dating from the late 19th century and now part of a prisoner of war complex. First impressions were appalling – the place was damp, cold, smelly and lice-ridden and there was limited access to fresh air or sunlight in the grim subterranean interior. The inevitable result of the poor conditions and inadequate diet was malnutrition and illness.

Conditions slowly began to improve and when the German authorities became convinced that the reports from Canada were inaccurate, the prisoners were returned to Spangenberg by the summer. Before long, rumours began to spread of another imminent move, this time to Oflag VIB at Warburg, a very large camp in Westphalia between Hanover and Düsseldorf with accommodation for at least 2,600 prisoners.

The transfer took place on 16 September 1941 and if the prisoners had hoped for some improvements in their conditions they were sadly disappointed, for one of their guards even admitted that Warburg was 'a very, very bad camp'.[4] In the usual British way the prisoners made the best of what they had and if anything escape activities took on an even greater intensity with several attempts although there were no successful 'home-runs'. It seems that Lawrence Edwards played his part in tunnelling schemes although as far as is known did not participate in an actual escape.[5]

One positive aspect of the size of the camp was a football pitch and reasonable sports facilities, encouraged by the presence of a number of former professional sportsmen in the camp, including Lawrence Edwards, Derek Heaton-Nichols, who had played cricket and rugby for Natal, and Colin MacLachlan, a Midland Counties rugby and association football player. Douglas Bader, the legless fighter pilot, was another notable prisoner at Warburg who provided much mirth in his favourite sport of 'goon-baiting', to the extreme exasperation of the German authorities at the camp.

In the meantime Göring was planning a special 'model' camp for captured Allied air force and Fleet Air Arm personnel, to be under the control of the Luftwaffe, and this opened in March 1942 as Stalag Luft III at Sagan in Poland, some 100 miles south-east of Berlin. It is not entirely clear whether Lawrence Edwards was in the first batch moved from Warburg to the new camp in May 1942, a group which included Douglas Bader, or if he was transported with several other RAF prisoners to temporary accommodation at Oflag XXIB at Schubin, another army-run camp also in Poland and about 37 miles from Thorn.

In any case Schubin was cleared in April 1943 and we know that Edwards was in Stalag Luft III at the time or very soon after the North Compound was opened for British airmen on 29 March 1943. Eventually the camp was to house nearly 11,000 Allied airmen, including 2,500 RAF personnel, and about 7,500 Americans.

The camp was immortalised in the famous 'Wooden Horse' escape from the East Compound in October 1943, when three prisoners used a gymnastic horse as cover for a tunnel near the perimeter fence, from which they exited the camp and made successful 'home runs' – the first successful escape from a camp which had been designed as 'escape-proof'.

Sadly this episode was overshadowed by the ill-fated 'Great Escape' of March 1944 in which a mass exodus was planned from the North Compound via an elaborate system of tunnels. Out of the 76 men who took part, three managed to reach home, 23 were recaptured and returned to Sagan, and the Gestapo rounded up and shot the remaining 50 escapers. Fortunately, although Edwards had been involved in previous escape activities there is no evidence that he was directly involved this time.

By this time arrangements were being made through the International Red Cross for repatriation to England. It is not entirely clear why Edwards was on the list for repatriation as he had by now largely recovered from his injuries. The fact that he had been such an early prisoner of war may well have played a part in the decision.[6] In any case he was transferred to Stalag IV D/Z and his passage was organised for return to England via Sweden on 26 September 1944, thus ending his five years as a prisoner of war.

Freedom and Home

On his return to England so close to the war's end there was no resumption of operational flying. Lawrence Edwards relinquished his commission in the RAF and was granted a temporary commission in the RNZAF as a

Flight Lieutenant prior to his return to New Zealand in March 1945. Now married, he continued his service career with a refresher flying course followed by various appointments as an adjutant, flying instructor and staff officer. At the same time he lost no time in getting back to the rugby field for at least two seasons culminating in selection for South Island's team, thus achieving the rare distinction of playing for both Islands. After he had hung up his rugby boots he continued as a selector for the RNZAF and retained an active involvement in the game.

The remainder of Lawrence Edwards' service career followed fairly conventional lines for a middle-ranking officer. By 1954 he was a squadron leader and an Honorary Aide-de-Camp to the Governor-General. His final appointment before retirement was as a wing commander and Officer Commanding the administrative functions of the RNZAF Station at Wigram. He was appointed an OBE in 1961 and retired from the Air Force in 1964. He died at home in Christchurch in July 1994 at the age of 81. One of his obituaries summed up the two distinguishing features of his career with the headline:

Stylish winger best known for fateful wartime flight

Notes:

LAURIE EDWARDS . . . fleet of foot

1   The names of his missing crewmen are inscribed on the Runnymede Memorial to the Missing.

2   The island of Norderney had featured in Erskine Childers' novel of 1903 *The Riddle of the Sands* (see Chapter 3 on the Darley brothers).

3   Quoted from *Freedom*, Wednesday 21 December 1955 (courtesy of The Alexander Turnbull Library, National Library of New Zealand, Wellington.)

4   Quoted from Charles Rollings, *Wire and Worse* p162.

5   Ibid. p264.

6   Charles Rollings maintains that it was often not clear why some prisoners were chosen for repatriation and not others (email to author 14/4/2010).

10

Basil Embry – Wartime Escaper
and Great Air Commander

Basil Embry was an outstanding wartime air commander who had the added distinction of making a daring escape from the Germans after being shot down during the battle of France in 1940.

Born in Gloucestershire in 1902 his first ambition was to join the Royal Navy but by the age of ten had set his sights on becoming a pilot. Granted a short service commission in the Royal Air Force in 1921 he began flying training at Netheravon in the Avro 504K, the workhorse of the RAF training schools of the day. From the start Embry was not interested in the quiet life and after a short period in No. 4 Squadron he requested an overseas posting and soon found himself with No. 45 Squadron in Turkey, followed by Iraq. During this period he flew some 70 operational missions and was awarded the AFC for his work, achieving a permanent commission in the meantime. Returning to the UK he became a flight commander at the Central Flying School at Netheravon in 1928 and it was here that he came under the influence of Marshal of the RAF Lord Trenchard, founder of the Royal Air Force. It was also at CFS that Embry first encountered David Atcherley (later Air Vice-Marshal D. F. W. Atcherley) as a pupil, one of the famed Atcherley brothers[1]. After graduating from RAF Staff College Embry was posted to RAF India, eventually taking up his first command, No. 20 Squadron, based in the North West Frontier Province of India. He returned to England in 1939 as a wing commander, having been awarded the first of his four DSOs for leadership.

At this point Embry realised how out of touch he was with recent aircraft developments and characteristically took an intensive training course in no fewer than 12 new types of aircraft. After a spell in the Air Ministry, on the outbreak of war he lobbied hard for a return to active operations and was given command of No. 21 Squadron, a posting immediately changed to No. 107 Squadron based at Wattisham, part of No. 2 Group, the squadron which had taken part in the first Allied bombing raid of the war and was later to be based at Great Massingham. Equipped with the Blenheim IV the squadron made many daring daylight bombing raids over enemy territory, and determined to lead by example, Embry

The flight was arranged by courtesy of the
DOWTY GROUP.

These covers were flown over the epic escape
route followed by Wg. Cdr. B.E. EMBRY, after
his BLENHEIM Mk. 4 was shot down by flak,
and he was captured near ST. OMER on the
27th May 1940. He escaped on the 29th May,
and made his way on foot via HESDIN, DREUIL-
HAMIL, CAYEUX, NEUFCHATEL, BEAUVAIS
and arrived in PARIS on the 18th June. Using
various modes of transport the Wg. Cdr.
eventually returned to England nearly 10 weeks
after leaving Wattisham, travelling via Limoges,
Marseilles and Spain.

A/C   KingAir A.100 – GBBVM.
Crew   Captain D.J. Fulluck,
           F.O. J.S. Merredew.
Flt. time 2hrs. 55 mins.
Route   Staverton–Le Bourget–Gatwick–
           Staverton

*Thirtieth Anniversary of the RAF Escaping Society First Day Post Office Cover:
Basil Embry's escape from France.*

rejected the convention that commanding officers should restrict their operational flying, and was soon engaged in a number of hazardous operations over France and the Low Countries and in April 1940 on raids to Stavanger at the start of the Norwegian campaign. It was during the bitterly fought Norwegian campaign in which he carried out ten raids on Stavanger airfield in eight days that resulted in the award of the first bar to his DSO for distinguished leadership.

On 28 May 1940 Embry was appointed to command RAF West Raynham in the rank of Acting Group Captain, the official theory being that he would now be forced to take more of a 'back seat' after the exceptional number of operations he had led. This was not quite his style, and he became the best commanding officer that West Raynham NEVER had, as on the day of his appointment he decided to accompany his squadron for the last time on an operation to bomb targets near St Omer, in order to introduce the new commanding officer Wing Commander L. R. Stokes to operational flying. It was an ill-fated decision as his aircraft was shot down on leaving the target. The air gunner Corporal Lang was killed but Embry with his navigator Whiting managed to bale out but were soon captured. He was forced to join a column of prisoners of war on the march and

Air Chief Marshal Sir Basil Embry
KCB, KBE, DSO, DFC, AFC.

although wounded in the leg was suddenly inspired by a signpost with the direction 'Embry, 3 kilometres'. He broke away only to be recaptured after a short spell of freedom. After another two breaks in the course of which he killed a German soldier he finally reached Paris, only to witness the arrival of Hitler in the French capital. After many adventures he made the 700 mile journey to freedom across France and Spain, eventually reaching England nine weeks and five days after being shot down. The entire story was related in his own account *Mission Completed*, published in 1957, and in *Wingless Victory* by Anthony Richardson, first published in 1950. It was poignant that in later years Embry kept in touch with the village priest and family who had sheltered him in France and even invited the family to stay with him at the headquarters in Stanmore when he was a staff officer after the war.

After his return to England and active service he took up a number of staff appointments but once again, eager to return to front-line operations, he reverted to the rank of Wing Commander to take command of a night fighter wing based at Rochford, near Southend in Essex. Towards the end of 1941 he was appointed to command RAF Wittering, once again playing a full part in operations. During this period he spent some time attached to the Desert Air Force as an adviser both in the Middle East and for a short time in Malta.

By the start of 1943 he was again on the staff of Fighter Command before being appointed Air Officer Commanding (AOC) of No. 2 Group on 1 June in the rank of Acting Air Vice-Marshal, only days before the Group was transferred from Bomber Command to the newly formed Second Tactical Air Force. From the Group HQ at Bylaugh Hall, near Dereham in Norfolk, Embry was tasked with carrying out air operations in the build up to Operation 'Overlord', the Allied invasion of Europe. Once again he was determined to lead from the front, and not only flew personally on as many operations as possible but ordered his staff to do so as well, including even the chaplains, claiming that this would improve the general morale of the Group. The enemy had put a price on his head as he had escaped from captivity and killed a German soldier, so he always assumed the identity of 'Wing Commander Smith'. He worked closely with David Atcherley, as Group Senior Air Staff Officer, to plan precision attacks on targets in enemy territory, and both flew together on a number of operations.

In October 1943 the Group carried out several attacks on power stations between Paris and Nantes, in which a future Prime Minister of France, M. Mendès-France took part, then a navigator with No. 342 (Lorraine) Squadron based at Hartford Bridge in Hampshire, and previously at Sculthorpe and Great Massingham. There was little that escaped Embry's attention as a commander. On the return trip from France on one operation with David Atcherley, flying at 50 feet over the Channel, they hit a large duck which damaged the aircraft. Embry sought out Peter Scott the naturalist to enquire into the migratory habits of ducks in order to reduce the risk of it happening again to any of his aircraft. Embry also recruited skilled model-makers to create detailed models of potential targets for the benefit of crews. Other targets included V-weapon sites in northern France and later, Gestapo headquarters in France and Denmark. It was during this time that Embry worked closely with Group Captain Percy 'Pick' Pickard, the commander of No. 140 Wing based at Sculthorpe, and later the commander of the Amiens Prison raid in early 1944. Pickard was a commander in exactly the same mould as Embry, and the latter was deeply disappointed to be refused permission to command the Amiens Prison raid which as it turned out was led by Pickard in February 1944 but from which he failed to return[2]. Embry did however succeed later in leading the raid on the Aarhus Gestapo Prison in Copenhagen, Denmark.

In January 1944 the Group Headquarters moved from Bylaugh Hall to Mongewell Park House in Berkshire, to be nearer target locations in northern Europe.

After the war's end Embry took up a number of RAF training and staff positions until his appointment as AOC-in-C Fighter Command in 1949, and then C-in-C Allied Forces Central Europe under NATO in 1953. He failed to achieve the appointment of Chief of the Air Staff which would have been the pinnacle of his career but there was no doubt that his greatest

Bylaugh Hall, near Dereham, Norfolk. Headquarters of No. 2 Group RAF from July 1943 to January 1944 and of No. 100 (Bomber Support) Group from January 1944 to December 1945. (author)

strength was as an operational commander. He retired from the RAF in 1955 in the rank of Air Chief Marshal. He died in Australia in 1977.

As a rather sad postscript to this remarkable career Basil Embry's medals were sold in a London auction on 19 April 2007. The collection realised a value of £155,350 and included the Distinguished Service Order (DSO) with three bars, the Distinguished Flying Cross (DFC), the Air Force Cross (AFC), the Grand Cross of the Order of the Bath (GCB) and the Knight Commander of the Order of the British Empire (KBE). Also included were awards from France, Iraq, Denmark and the Netherlands, Embry's air chief marshal's ceremonial sword and mementoes including his flying logbooks.

Notes:

[1] Air Vice-Marshal D. F. W. Atcherley CB, CBE, DSO, DFC was killed flying a Meteor in 1952.

[2] John Reed in *After the Battle* journal No.28 gives a full account of Operation 'Jericho' and Basil Embry's role.

11

Percy Charles Pickard – Bomber Pilot and Amiens Prison Raid Hero

Pickard was an exceptional operational pilot in World War Two who was the 'star' of the wartime film 'Target for Tonight' and was later killed in leading the famous Mosquito raid on the Gestapo Prison at Amiens in early 1944.

Born in 1915 he was educated at Framlingham College in Suffolk, and spent some time in Kenya on a friend's farm before returning to England to volunteer for the Army. He was rejected for officer training as being 'too dim', so chose the RAF instead and trained to be a pilot, becoming commissioned as Acting Pilot Officer in 1937. His first posting was to No. 214 Squadron at Feltwell, flying Handley Page Harrow bombers. In the meantime he had married Dorothy Hodgkin and at the same time formed what was to be a lifelong relationship with her old English sheepdog 'Ming'. By 1940 he was based at Newmarket flying Wellingtons with No. 99 Squadron, where he teamed up with his navigator Sergeant (later Flight Lieutenant) Alan Broadley, with whom he would serve throughout the war. Pickard and his crew survived a ditching in the North Sea on 19 June 1940 after their Wellington O-Orange had been damaged over the Ruhr. They landed in the middle of a minefield and it was thanks to the rescue boats from RAF Felixstowe and the crew of the Gorleston Lifeboat *Louis Stephens* that they were picked up. It was at this time that Dorothy noticed a kind of 'sixth sense' that Ming had developed whenever Pickard was flying on operations and was in any kind of trouble. The dog would sit out of doors scanning the sky and would only rest when Pickard had safely returned, as was proved by Dorothy checking the timings of the aircraft's return.

In July 1940 Pickard was posted to command No. 311 (Czech) Squadron at East Wretham and was invited to star in the Government propaganda film 'Target for Tonight', aimed at showing the British public how Bomber Command was hitting back at Germany. He became known for his call-sign 'F for Freddie' which he retained up to his final flight. His service with the Czechs earned him his first DSO, which also brought in his honour an extra day's holiday for his old school at Framlingham College.

Percy 'Pick' Pickard (centre) as CO of No. 161 Squadron at Tempsford, with Lysander in background. 'Ming' the old English sheepdog foreground left. (Framlingham College)

Moving to No. 51 Squadron at Dishforth to fly Whitley bombers he was soon engaged in high level photography rather than bombing. In February 1942 while at Dishforth, he personally transported the commandos by Whitley bomber on the Bruneval Raid, an operation to dismantle German radar installations in northern France. The mission was a great success and Pickard was awarded a bar to his DSO for the part he played – yet another extra day's holiday being enjoyed by his old school!

Later that year he took command of No. 161 Squadron at Tempsford to engage in risky and difficult clandestine operations, conveying secret agents of SOE (Special Operations Executive) to occupied France. The agents would first be billeted locally and then transported to farm buildings – later called 'Gibraltar Farm' – within the bounds of RAF Tempsford. Then the party would be flown to France and either dropped by parachute over a pre-arranged point or transported by Lysander and 'hedge-hopped' to a local field well away from the prying eyes of the Germans. Either way considerable luck and cool nerve was required by pilot and crew which was borne out on one occasion when Pickard's Lysander was bogged down in mud in a French field near Tournais after picking up a group of agents, and it took over two hours for local villagers to dislodge the aircraft ready for take-off. His work with the squadron earned him a second bar to his DSO, to the delight of Framlingham pupils.

In July 1943 Pickard was posted to command RAF Sculthorpe where No. 140 Wing was established consisting of three squadrons, Nos 464 (RAAF), 487 (RNZAF) and 21 Squadrons, soon to be equipped with the Mosquito fighter bomber. The Wing was part of No. 2 Group of the Second Tactical Air Force commanded by the legendary Air Vice-Marshal Basil Embry (see previous chapter) who had earlier spotted Pickard's outstanding record as an operational commander. The Mosquito was proving itself an exceptional and versatile aircraft in striking at special targets of importance like Gestapo headquarters, V-bomb sites and power stations, a role pioneered at nearby RAF Marham when Mosquitoes had raided Berlin in daylight on 30 January 1943 on the occasion of Hitler's birthday. Pickard had a narrow escape when his Mosquito 'F for Freddie' was seriously damaged by flak when attacking Pont Château power station at low level. He made it to Predannack

Pickard and Flt Lt John Broadley (navigator) in front of 'F' for Freddie at Hunsdon, January 1944. Both were killed the following month. (After the Battle)

Mosquitoes setting out on the raid 18 February 1944. Both aircraft in picture from No. 464 Sqn returned safely. (After the Battle)

in Cornwall on one engine and was confident enough to risk returning to Sculthorpe after a brief inspection of the damage.

Pickard's fame and that of the Mosquito brought an unexpected visitor to Sculthorpe during the winter of 1943, Wing Commander Leonard Cheshire, commanding officer of No. 617 'Dam Busters' Squadron. It was speculated that Cheshire was considering a Christmas drop of food and clothes to his brother's prisoner of war camp at Sagan (Stalag Luft III) in Poland and was well aware of Pickard's experience in secret operations, but more likely he was evaluating the Mosquito's potential in precision target-marking.

By the end of 1943 the Wing was moved to Hunsdon near old Harlow in Hertfordshire, to be closer to French targets and it was from there that Pickard's final operation was flown, Operation 'Jericho', to free French prisoners of the Gestapo from Amiens Prison on 18 February 1944. News had reached London that some 120 prisoners were facing execution at or near 19 February and apart from the humanitarian concern this was a vital mission to prevent the collapse of the French Resistance network in the area in the months leading to Allied landings on the continent. The Germans had even dug a mass grave in preparation for the impending executions. There was no time to lose but the weather on the appointed day was appalling, with frequent snow showers. The task was to fly as low as 25 feet to deliver delay-action bombs to enable to prisoners to escape uninjured, at the same time attempting to destroy the German quarters.

The raid was a success although Pickard's aircraft was shot down while circling to observe the results of the attack and he was killed along with Broadley. They were buried in St Pierre Cemetery, Amiens. On his headstone the decorations 'VC, DSO, DFC Bars' were added to Pickard's name – the French mistakenly adding the 'VC' and mixing up the Bars – if only showing the high regard they had for Pickard's bravery. However, the Air Ministry later requested that the letters 'VC' be removed and the proposal by the French to make a posthumous award to Pickard with their highest decorations of the Companion of the Légion d'Honneur and the Croix de Guerre was also turned down on the grounds that foreign posthumous awards could not be granted. The raid itself led to the deaths of 102 prisoners but 258 managed to escape including 12 of the group due to be shot the next day, and 50 Germans were killed. A post-war analysis of the raid concluded that 'The attack on Amiens prison will remain one of the RAF's epics.'[1]

The postscript to the story was that Ming, the old English sheepdog, had been left at Sculthorpe in the charge of Pickard's second-in-command.

Pickard's grave in St Pierrre Cemetery, Amiens, before headstone in place. Note 'VC' inscription which was later removed. (After the Battle)

On the afternoon of the 18th Dorothy, Pickard's wife, received a phone call saying that the dog had become seriously ill. She immediately rushed to Sculthorpe and when she saw the comatose state of the animal she knew then that Pickard had been killed. Her fears were later confirmed. It took a month for the dog to recover its health.

Later Dorothy moved to Rhodesia with her family and Ming. In 1951 the old dog was in such poor health that she became very weak until one night she appeared to want to get outside into the garden. Dorothy recalled the many occasions Ming had done this when Pickard was flying on operations, and the dog would watch the sky for hours on end. This time she went outside, the sound of a whistle was heard (although nobody was present) and the dog looked up to the sky and then collapsed and died.

Pickard was a great British hero who is rightly commemorated at his old school as an inspiration to present and future generations. Basil Embry summed up his achievements: 'In courage, devotion to duty, fighting spirit and powers of really leading, Percy Pickard stood out as one of the great airmen of the war and as a shining example of British manhood. I always felt he was part of a character from an earlier Elizabethan age.' In recent days his family and others have demanded that the French decorations at last be granted, as stated in a *Daily Express* article of 7 April 2004 by Katie Fraser in which his nephew remarked that Pickard 'embodied the consummate English gentleman, brave, kind, honourable and loyal'.

Note:
[1] John Reed in *After the Battle* journal No. 28 gives a full account of Operation 'Jericho'.

12

Henry Labouchere – A Norfolk Life in Aviation

Henry Labouchere has lived most of his life with aeroplanes and has amassed to date around 7,000 flying hours on 157 types of aircraft. A Norfolk man from a long-standing Norfolk family, he was born in 1948 at Sculthorpe where his grandfather had been vicar, having served as a curate at Burnham Thorpe. His father was an army officer who had bought the rectory at Sculthorpe on his retirement, which remained Henry's home until 1968.

By his own admission schooling was not a success, first at the Dragon School in Oxford where his school reports were anything but promising. His history master commented: 'If ignorance is bliss, then this child must be truly happy' and his French master wrote: 'This term's work has been effortless, in every sense of the word'. Nothing daunted, he then moved on to Grenville College in Bideford, north Devon, where once again academic success eluded him and although he enjoyed activities like boating he was soon to leave 'after a contretemps with management'.

Returning to Norfolk he attended first the Norfolk School of Agriculture and then King's Lynn Technical College (now the College of West Anglia).

He started flying at the age of eight with his brother, his senior by ten years and a pilot in the Royal Air Force. Allied to that was the fact that their house was sited at the end of the Sculthorpe airfield runway during the years of the Cold War in the early 1950s, when there were American B-36s, B-66s, B-45s, Fairchild Packets, T-33s by the dozen, and lots of C-47s (Dakotas) – in short the skies were filled with aircraft. He recalled a B-66 crash at Barsham. After the Americans left, the Jaguars moved in from Coltishall for a while and then some old Sabres were dumped there for disposal.

Henry thought about joining the Army Air Corps but in the end opted for freelance flying with Tiger Moths of the McAully Flying Group at Little Snoring. Formerly known as the Fakenham Flying Group, it had been formed in 1957 with the aim of providing affordable flying in north Norfolk and therefore encouraging aviation in the region. The Group was renamed the McAully Flying Group in memory of Elwyn 'Mac' McAully, the founder member who was killed at Little Snoring in 1960 while practising for an aerobatic display. Damage to the hangars from gales meant that the aircraft were only partly sheltered from the weather and were nearly always wet. It was at Little Snoring that Henry was taught to fly by Barry Tempest, his boss, in about 1965-66, although he did not actually qualify for his licence there because 'once I'd been solo there that was it – I didn't need to know any more'.

He then joined Westwick Aviation at Ludham, which had a fleet of crop-spraying aeroplanes including Tiger Moths, for example G-APIG, soon to be replaced by Pawnees like G-ASKV, G-AWFS, G-ASLA and G-ATER. There was also a Cub G-AVOO. 'We used to spray death and destruction all over East Anglia, Lancashire and Scotland, a wonderful job but we never got any money – a good break into aviation.'

Eventually lack of money forced Henry to go to Australia – he went from earning £12 to £13 for a 90-hour week to $100, about the same as £100 in England. His first job was in Perth and far removed from flying, painting white lines on the highway. He then obtained a truck driver's licence before moving to south Australia where he qualified for his pilot's licence, his first task being to ferry an aircraft to Indonesia – a bit tricky for the inexperienced! Various jobs followed including a year with Freeport, Indonesia, flying and maintaining a Catalina Flying Boat. In the meantime in 1970 he had bought a Tiger Moth, originally VH-WAL and now registered G-BEWN, which he has owned ever since.

Returning to England in 1976 he took up a number of flying jobs including film work. One of the first was flying a DC3 (Dakota) in *A Bridge Too Far*, which in his view should have been called 'An Hour Too Long'. Other films included *The Eagle Has Landed* and *A Man Called Intrepid* at Little Rissington in Gloucestershire where he met up with David Niven. He came across Harrison Ford while working on the film *Hanover Street* once again at Little Rissington, and later at Bovingdon in Hertfordshire. Other actors he has known from the filming world included the late Christopher Reeve. In between times he went to Africa flying DC3s in Khartoum, not a job which he particularly enjoyed.

By the mid-1980s he set up in business at the former RAF airfield of Langham on the north Norfolk coast – inspection, repair, overhaul, maintenance and rebuilding aircraft – an MOT station for aeroplanes. He still undertakes flying jobs in various parts of the country in aircraft which include a DH Rapide at the Shuttleworth Collection in Old Warden and a DH Dragon. His jobs include trips to the north of Scotland, to Blair Atholl and Perth and throughout Europe, for example, to Poland.

Going further afield a memorable flight was one of the longest (and slowest) ever, from Mildenhall to Melbourne in a DH 80A Puss Moth (G-AAZP) on 21 October 1984, when he flew with owner Tim Williams on the 50th Anniversary of the 1934 MacRobertson air race from England to Australia. The original race had been one of the great events in the aviation calendar at the time, in front of 60,000 spectators at the newly opened RAF Mildenhall and the distance to be covered totalled 11,300 miles. The winners on this occasion were C. W. A. Scott and Tom Campbell Black in their scarlet DH88 Comet Racer G-ACSS *Grosvenor House* (now preserved at the Shuttleworth Collection). Incidentally another of the original competitors were husband and wife Jim Mollison and Amy Johnson, also in a Comet Racer, but they failed to complete the race owing to mechanical problems. On the Anniversary event Henry Labouchere and Tim Williams'

Poster advertising the Mildenhall to Melbourne Air Race of 20 October 1934.

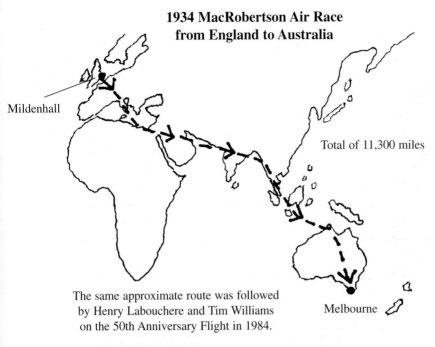

1934 MacRobertson Air Race
from England to Australia

Mildenhall

Total of 11,300 miles

The same approximate route was followed
by Henry Labouchere and Tim Williams
on the 50th Anniversary Flight in 1984.

Melbourne

Puss Moth was one of 21 machines from the De Havilland Moth Club taking part in front of around 300 spectators, carrying a message from the Lord Mayor of London to the Lord Mayor of Melbourne. The starting flag was raised by Air Vice-Marshal Donald Bennett, who had flown a Lockheed Special Vega in the original race before becoming the Pathfinder Bomber chief in World War Two.

In 1996 Henry and Sir Torquil Norman flew a DH Dragonfly (G-AEDU) to the Oshkosh air show in Wisconsin:

'Torquil Norman is a wonderful man and we get on well together. We have done trips to Australia and New Zealand, mostly in Tiger Moths.' Torquil Norman had joined the Fleet Air Arm after the war and flew Sea Furies from aircraft carriers. At six foot four inches in height he was too tall for the six foot two inches' maximum height allowed, and had to obtain specially large trousers to enable him to bend his knees so that he could pass the medical. Later he joined No. 601 Squadron RAF with his two brothers, the only squadron in which there were three brothers serving at the same time. After National Service he worked in international banking and later became a leading businessman in the toy industry. Since retirement he has been very active in charities for young people.

The Oshkosh trip was an ambitious flight in more senses than one, not only financially but for 'the price they charged for gin and tonics in Greenland'. Also in a flight like that 'you only have 260 hp and a couple of old engines there and you are in the land of no second chances. We had a 68-gallon tank on the seat which gave us about 11 hours' endurance (normally the aeroplane has only about six hours) and we only did about 100 knots. We went via the west coast of Scotland where we had very rough weather, then to Stornoway, Reykjavik in Iceland and Greenland – very desolate there. We then climbed to about 11,000 feet to scrape over the top of the ice-cap and then there was a delay for several days because of bad weather.'

After Baffin Island they ran into 'horrifying' weather until eventually reaching Goose Bay and then Portland Main. Over Ohio there were problems with oil pressure in an engine and Torquil landed the machine on one engine at Tiffin in Ohio. By that time they were too late for the display at Oshkosh. On the trip home, they decided on the long route from Goose Bay to Reykjavik, each leg about 640 miles in total:

'We did get quite iced up at one stage and came out of the cloud. Luckily there was a raging 50-knot wind underneath us which was causing a lot of salt spray off the waves and when we got down low all the salt got onto the aeroplane and got the ice off (which isn't in the PPL handbook* of how to de-ice your aeroplane). It worked. So we flew along in the salt spray and found the fjord, landed and poured ourselves triples which cost a fortune. Next day we fired up and because of the fuel load we couldn't make it to 6,000 feet and took the long way around, going through a couple of fronts on the way to Iceland. The aircraft was a difficult one to fly on instruments so it was easier to fly low over the ocean at 30 feet and do the radio by relays to airliners. From Greenland we went to Glasgow and Langham in a day – 11 hours. We landed here and poured ourselves another triple! Quite an interesting trip.'

For this long east-west transatlantic flight in a vintage aeroplane both men were awarded the Certificate of Merit from the Royal Aero Club.

Henry attends various events connected with the Tiger Moth, like the 70th Anniversary gathering at Cambridge Airport on 26 January 2008 where he provided an aerobatic display. He tends to do less aerobatics these days: 'Aerobatics in a Tiger Moth is like trying to steeplechase a cow and at 70 years' old now they need treating with a great deal of respect. I do the odd roll but that is about it.' He has had a few crashes or as he puts it rather more take-offs to his credit than landings mostly due to engines stopping, for example in a Fox Moth, and on one occasion in a Pawnee:

'In this job you get an engine failure about every thousand hours. These are old engines, not as reliable as modern car engines, but invariably you can put the machine down somewhere. The more experience you have the less you worry when it happens. The first couple of times it happens you just want to call on the radio for help and hope that some big hook will haul you up but it doesn't happen and you are on your own. If I have an engine failure that is the last thing I would do, unless I am over the ocean. If I am over land I make sure I don't hit the nearside hedge at 70 knots, rather the far side one at 10 knots!'

Choosing a favourite aircraft to fly was difficult – 'How many am I allowed?' His all-time favourite is the Mosquito – like those based at Langham during the 1950s:

'After that I would probably choose a Cessna 180 or the Leopard Moth – the latter is a fantastic aeroplane that flies in all weathers, superbly efficient, made in 1932 or 1933. It can fold up and go into the garage. The Cessna 180s and 185s were built in 1952, and they are about as practical as you can get – a great cruising speed and able to take off in a couple of hundred yards. I also like the DC3 although I don't often fly them now. The biggest aircraft I ever flew was a Boeing 707, a coal-burning one, with black smoke pouring out. That was when I was working in Khartoum flying DC3s – not a favourite job at the time.'

Of the people Henry has known connected with aviation one of the most memorable was the late Alex Henshaw, the famous Spitfire test pilot, who came to fly the Tiger Moth, an added bonus being that Alex loved the DH Leopard Moth and Henry had one at Langham (G-ACOJ). There was a family connection as Alex's father ran a fertiliser business and used to do business with Henry's father–in-law. Alex Henshaw had joined Vickers Armstrong at the outbreak of the Second World War initially testing Wellingtons and subsequently the Spitfire and Walrus. He was appointed Chief Test Pilot at Castle Bromwich, Birmingham, in June 1940. He died in 2007 at the age of 94.

Another contact with historic aviation is the original Gypsy Racing Moth G-AAXG which has recently been at the back of the hangar at Langham. Once the property of Sir Alan Butler, its present owner is Simon Kidston, son of the aviator Lieutenant-Commander Kidston. The aeroplane's logbook traces the first 15 minute flight by Alan Butler at Stag Lane in June 1930 to racing venues around Europe, then export to New Zealand in 1935 before the machine ended up in France until being purchased by the Kidston family. Although much modified, it retains the white ensign on its tail which dates back to 1935.

Sir Alan Butler is the man credited with coming to the aid of the fledgling de Havilland Company in the early 1920s after a chance meeting with Geoffrey de Havilland to place an order for a private aeroplane. The outcome was that Butler was so impressed with the company's work that he invested much needed capital in the enterprise and became chairman in 1924. The consequence was that de Havillands were able to do much more experimental work, without which we might never have had one of the greatest warplanes ever produced, the de Havilland Mosquito.

The former Langham Airfield provides the background to Henry Labouchere's work and he is more than conscious of its historic setting. He has teamed up with fellow enthusiasts to form the Friends of Langham Dome, one of the few remaining airfield buildings surviving on the site which was used to train anti-aircraft gunners. The aim is to raise money to restore the building and preserve it for future generations. He is keen to make contact with those who had personal experience of the building and the function it served. Henry Labouchere is a man of modest ambitions, content with the life he shares with his wife Jill and daughters Lucy and Henrietta. His aim is to keep healthy so that he can keep flying!

Friends of Langham Dome website:
www.langhamdometrainer.co.uk

Extracts from conversations with Henry Labouchere, Friday 23 Jan. 2009, Saturday 1 May and Tuesday 3 August 2010 at Langham.

*PPL = Private Pilots' Licence

Tiger Moth G-BEWN (formerly VH-WAL) at Langham.

Alex Henshaw with Henry Labouchere's Tiger Moth

13

Wing Commander Ken Wallis –
Norfolk's Very Own Flying Legend

Wing Commander Ken Wallis is one of the great aviators of his generation, widely known and appreciated within the UK and in many other countries. His career in aviation has spanned almost the entire history of flight – he is well into his seventieth decade as a qualified pilot. Ian Hancock of the Norfolk and Suffolk Aviation Museum has described this remarkable career in *The Lives of Ken Wallis*, now in its fifth edition.

Born in Ely in 1916 Ken had an early introduction to engineering and aviation. His father and uncle had started a motorcycle manufacturing business and were so inspired by the pioneering flights of the Wright brothers and Blériot that they decided to have a go at building their own flying machine. The result was the Wallbro' Monoplane (the name Wallbro' being

short for the Wallis Brothers). Unusually the fuselage frame and wings were made from steel tubing rather than the conventional wooden framing of machines at the time, and advertised as 'the first aeroplane to be built in Cambridge'. The first flight was made on 4 July 1910 and a number of other successful if short flights were made during that summer, although there were a few minor mishaps in the process. Unfortunately the aircraft was eventually wrecked in its shed during a freak storm later in 1910, which ended this bold and enterprising experiment at least for the time being.

'Wallbro' poster, 1910. Ken's father and uncle later discovered to their horror that the 'All British' description was not strictly true as the engine had a German magneto!

– 156 –

It was not the end of the story for Ken took up the challenge of building a replica of the machine (G-BFIP) and flying it from RAF Swanton Morley in August 1978. Thereafter the aeroplane was displayed at the Norfolk & Suffolk Aviation Museum at Flixton, where on 4 July 2010 the centenary of its first flight was celebrated with Ken, President of the Museum, as guest of honour.

Ken's flying career began in fits and starts having been rejected by the Royal Air Force Volunteer Reserve (RAFVR) in 1936 owing to a defect in one eye, but in April of the following year managed to qualify for his 'A' Licence with the Cambridge Aero Club – with a total of 12 hours 10 minutes on DH Moths. Needing to maintain his hours he switched for a time to flying a BAC 'Drone', a glider powered by a motorcycle engine mounted above the wing, for the princely sum of 7s 6d per hour.

He had another go at applying for the Air Force, this time for a short service commission, but was once again turned down on the same grounds as before. Not inclined to give up easily he took advantage of a new scheme called the Civil Air Guard by which flying tuition was offered at an affordable price to 'air-minded persons' with successful candidates going

Ken Wallis flew the 'Wallbro' replica from Swanton Morley in August 1978. (Norfolk and Suffolk Aviation Museum).

forward as potential RAFVR aircrew in the event of war. Through the scheme he was able to hire a Gypsy Moth for 2s 6d per hour – not a bad bargain if one considers that only a few years earlier Cobham's Flying Circus was charging anything between 2s 6d and 5s per hour for a flight. In the event Ken was third time lucky and proceeded to flying training after a short period on what was termed 'deferred service' owing to the shortage of qualified instructors and places at flying training schools. He managed to pass the eye test by turning his head sideways and using his good eye to read the test chart, while the doctor was looking at the chart.

Ken's first operational posting was to No. 268 Army Co-operation Squadron at Westley in Suffolk flying Lysanders followed by a spell with No. 241 Squadron at Inverness. The main task was to take off before dawn and fly around the coast to detect any sign of the expected invasion fleet. However, in June 1941 he transferred to Bomber Command, converting to the twin-engined Vickers Wellington at Lossiemouth in Scotland. Then followed a posting to No. 103 Squadron first at Newton near Nottingham, shortly moving on to Elsham Wolds in Lincolnshire.

Ken's tour on an operational bomber squadron produced many dangerous moments and lucky escapes and he lost many of his friends. On

'Wallbro' replica at the Museum.

the night of 20/21 September 1941 he and his crew were returning from a raid to Frankfurt, where they had been unable to find the target owing to cloud cover and had then been diverted to the secondary target of bombing invasion barges along the Dutch coast. Low on fuel they discovered that the home airfield was fog-bound as was the diversion airfield of Binbrook. By the time they were over the airfield there was no fuel showing on the gauges and Ken made several unsuccessful attempts to land. On climbing the aircraft out the engines stopped and he gave the order to bail out and although the aircraft was by this time descending rapidly there was just sufficient height for the crew to escape. With the crew out of the aircraft Ken struggled for the exit, only to find at the last minute that the required harness was separated from the parachute pack. With barely seconds to spare and at the minimal height of 700 feet, he sorted out the equipment and jumped, hitting the ground hard and suffering concussion and a back injury. A spell in hospital followed and he became a member of the Caterpillar Club, the select band of aircrew who have survived a parachute descent to save their lives.

Only a month later Ken's Wellington was struck by lightning on the way to Mannheim in appalling weather. They struggled home in the face of serious icing problems which were affecting the engines and found themselves being shot at by the Harwich batteries (a not uncommon RAF experience) as they crossed the coast. Over Immingham Docks the aircraft collided with the Humber balloon barrage, designed to prevent the Luftwaffe making low bombing runs. The port wing and engine were severely damaged and Ken had to make an emergency crash landing at his home base, escaping with only minor injuries. One bonus was that the crew were invited to a party the following day laid on by Balloon Command at Grimsby. It turned out that the balloons had succeeded in bringing down seven German aircraft as against 42 of the RAF!

On the night of 21 January 1942 in an early experiment which was to lead to the formation of the Pathfinder Force of Bomber Command, the target was Bremen for which they carried a full bomb load of incendiaries. Beneath them on the bomb racks were four and a half inch reconnaissance flares to be dropped from Emden to Bremen on parachutes to light the way to the target.

The navigator selected to drop the first flare but it was not seen to ignite. He asked again for 'Bomb Doors Open' and dropped the second flare. There was then an explosion in the bomb bay which blew the forward plywood bulkhead into the cockpit, with enormous white light and smoke. A reconnaissance flare and its parachute had been retained by the iced-up bomb doors and the intense heat of the magnesium ignited the incendiary bomb load. The load was jettisoned, bashing open the bomb doors but the Wellington burned underneath for some time. On return to base the crew discovered that the magnesium had melted the bomb bay beams and they were lucky that the fire had only been inches away from the fuel pipes.

During off-duty periods Ken was having regular dates with a young WAAF Section Officer called Peggy Stapley, in local watering holes like The Saracen's Head in Lincoln. She was based at Elsham Wolds. They decided to get married just after the expiry of his Bomber 'tour' on 29 April 1942. His best man was Pilot Officer Ken Winchester who had been his second pilot. Sadly he was killed on the night of 15/16 October 1942 during a raid on Cologne. Ken Wallis had five second pilots during the time of his bombing operations, all of whom became captains of their own crews. None survived. Ken commented that while there are many celebrations for 'The Battle of Britain' there are few to commemorate 'The Battle of Germany'. However, during the summer of 2010 plans have at long last been approved for a permanent Bomber Command Memorial to be sited in central London.

A posting followed to No. 21 Operational Training Unit at Moreton-in-the Marsh, Gloucestershire, where he flew a number of special operational missions. One of these involved flying an Anson over the usual routes taken by Wellington training aircraft over East Anglia and the North Sea, transmitting the different call-signs of the Wellington trainers to give the impression that normal training was going on. In the meantime the Wellington trainers were bombed-up and ready for the first Thousand Bomber raid to Cologne which took place on the night of 30/31 May 1942. Later in the war Ken served with No. 37 Squadron at Tortorella near Foggia in Italy, before being appointed a Flight Commander in the Central Gunnery School specialising in Air Armament.

By this time he had applied for a transfer to Mosquito night fighters and 'a night vision test was made on each eye and all hell was let loose when my defective right eye was checked!' He was whisked off to an appointment with the Air Commodore Livingston, the top RAF 'medic' in Bristol who said to him:

'Wallis, I'd rather have a man with a bit of fire in his belly who wants to fly than some of the perfect specimens I see who don't. I will prescribe for you a pair of goggles with a corrected lens for your bad eye. Don't have them on but always have them with you. If you get your good eye shot out on operations put the goggles on and bring the aircraft home!'

However, as it turned out Ken never got the chance to go to Mosquito night fighters and instead returned to bomber operations.

Eventually he applied for, and was granted, a permanent commission in the newly formed Technical Branch of the RAF to work on armament and ammunition design. By no means content to 'fly a desk' he maintained his flying hours in the years after the war and qualified for a 'Green' instrument rating on jets. He had a few narrow escapes, such as a forced landing he made while flying a Chipmunk from the airfield at Hendon. The engine cut at 300 feet after take-off close to trees and high tension cables. By skilful side-slipping he was able to bring the machine down safely next to a park bench occupied by mothers with babies in their prams! As a result of the episode Ken received a 'Green Endorsement' in his logbook for 'saving life and property by skilled judgement'.

One of the highlights of his post-war RAF service was a posting with Strategic Air Command of the US Air Force from 1956-58 based at Omaha, Nebraska, flying the giant Convair B-36 10-engined bombers, each

The Wallis Rolls-Royce 'Silver Ghost Special' at Offutt Air Force Base, US Air Force, Omaha, Nebraska, with Vickers Valiant XD818, the aircraft which dropped the 'H' Bomb on Christmas Island during Operation 'Grapple'. (Ken Wallis)

with a crew of 22 including four pilots and permanently armed with an atomic bomb. This was no rehearsal, as Ken testifies: 'We knew if we got the message, we were to attack Russia'.

There was also an opportunity to indulge his passion for cars, for he took to the States a Rolls-Royce Silver Ghost he had obtained and rebuilt as a 'special', where it caught the eye of none other than the legendary commander of Strategic Air Command General Curtis E. LeMay, who ordered Ken to take the take the car around various shows in the Mid West as a representative for the Command.

It was also during his posting in the United States that he came across a new type of 'gyroglider' being marketed by a Dr Igor Bensen. There were many features about the design he disliked and he determined to make of it something more practical and airworthy. When he returned to England he decided to make a powered version with a conventional control column and the eventual outcome was the design of the autogyro WA-116 which by 1962 had achieved a Civil Certificate of Airworthiness from the Ministry of Aviation. The potential of the aircraft was noticed by the Army Air Corps and Miles Brothers received a contract to build three autogyros for Army trials. These were 'open frame' versions which lacked a cockpit nacelle and the trials took place during the bitter winter months of 1962/63. The experience of the open cockpits of the machines was enough to persuade the Army to take up the helicopter option instead with the enclosed cabin.

After retiring from the RAF in 1964 Ken devoted his time to the development of the autogyro, using it in a large number of civil and military activities. These include police work, searches for missing persons including the famous Lord Lucan and scanning the landscape for buried bodies. Ken remains convinced of the untapped potential of the autogyro with its essential simplicity of design and economical running costs.

He has combined the roles of pilot, engineer, designer, inventor and ambassador for aviation in many countries of the world. One memorable event was his part in the 1967 James Bond film *You Only Live Twice* in which he acted as Sean Connery's double as James Bond in the aerial combat involving his autogyro 'Little Nellie' (which he built himself). In 2008-9 this episode featured in an exhibition at the Imperial War Museum dedicated to the author Ian Fleming. Ken has had many other film roles.

As the designer and builder of at least a dozen autogyros at his Norfolk estate, he has achieved around 17 world class records in the aircraft, in altitude, speed and distance. He was extremely frustrated when the Civil Aviation Authority (CAA) – or 'Campaign Against Aviation' as it has been termed, eventually refused to renew his flying licence for air displays purely on the grounds of his age, despite the fact that he is fitter than many 20 years younger than himself. However, he still flies around his own estate, although well into his 90s. In April 2009 the *Eastern Daily Press* reported that he was planning to beat his own world record for autogyros for the fastest flight over three km, which he previously completed at 129.1 mph. The only problem about this is that the CAA has imposed a speed limit for autogyros of 70 mph but there has been some flexibility shown about this rule.

His pioneering work with the autogyro has earned him the distinction of being a fellow of the Society of Experimental Test Pilots. He has also given much of his time to the promotion of aviation heritage, for example as a very active President of the Norfolk and Suffolk Aviation Museum. The Ken Wallis Hall at the Museum was officially opened by him on 4 July 2010 to exhibit the Wallbro' monoplane replica along with his memorabilia. He is also involved with many local causes and gives talks to associations and groups, usually without the aid of notes. Ken Wallis certainly more than fits the description of 'Norfolk's very own flying legend', according to the *Eastern Daily Press.* His main satisfaction is that he has continued the family tradition in aviation started by his father and uncle in 1900.

A Summary of the Awards and Achievements of Wing Commander K. H. Wallis MBE

1963   The Alan Marsh Medal – The Royal Aeronautical Society and The Helicopter Association of Great Britain.

1969   The Seagrave Trophy – The Royal Automobile Club and The Royal Aeronautical Society.

1973   The Breguet Trophy – The Aero Club of France and The Royal Aero Club.

1975   The Silver Medal – The Royal Aero Club.

1975   The Rose Trophy – The Helicopter Club of Great Britain.

1980   Honorary Fellowship – The Manchester Polytechnic.

1982   The Reginald Mitchell Trophy – Stoke on Trent Association of Engineers.

1984	The Rose Trophy – The Helicopter Club of Great Britain.
1985	The Seagrave Trophy – The Royal Automobile Club and the Royal Aeronautical Society.
1989	The Salomon Trophy – The Royal Aero Club.
1995	The FAI Gold Rotorcraft Medal – Fédération Aéronautique Internationale.
1996	Member of the British Empire (MBE) – For Services to Aviation.
1997	Honorary Doctorate of Engineering – University of Birmingham.
1998	Honorary Fellowship – Society of Experimental Test Pilots – For Lifetime Achievement as an Aeronautical Engineer, Pioneering the Many Uses of Autogyros.
1998	Guinness Book of World Records – The Oldest Aviator to set a World Record.
1999	Special Award – The Air League – For Record-Breaking Autogyro Developments.
1999	Sir Barnes Wallis Medal – The Guild of Air Pilots and Navigators – For Exceptional Contribution to Aviation Over More Than 50 Years.
2002	Honorary Doctorate – Hofstra University, New York, USA – For Accomplishments in Aviation.
2005	Pilcher Memorial Lecture Medal
2006	Honorary Fellowship – The Institute of Transport Administration.

World Records Recognised by
The Fédération Aéronautique Internationale

11.05.68	Altitude
12.05.69	Speed Over 3 Kilometres.
13.07.74	Distance In Closed Circuit Without Landing.
13.07.74	Speed Over 500 Kilometres Closed Circuit.
13.07.74	Speed Over 100 Kilometres Closed Circuit.
28.09.75	Non-Stop Distance In Straight Line*.
28.09.75	Duration*.
20.07.82	Altitude.
14.08.84	Speed Over 15 Kilometres*.
17.04.85	Speed Over 100 Kilometres Closed Circuit*.
18.09.86	Speed Over 3 Kilometres*.
05.08.88	Speed Over 1,000 Kilometres Closed Circuit*.

05.08.88   Speed Over 500 Kilometres Closed Circuit*.
05.08.88   Distance In Closed Circuit*.
06.12.90   Time To Climb To 3,000 Metres.
19.03,98   Time To Climb To 3,000 Metres*.
16.11.02   Speed Over 3 Kilometres* (129 mph).
* Ken Wallis holds these absolute World Records set in both classes of autogyro.

The FAI has awarded *Diplome de Record* in respect of the 34 World Records set by Ken Wallis in two classes of autogyro: Class E3 (any autogyro) and Class 3a (autogyro under 500 Kilos in weight).

Source of Summary of Awards and Achievements: Ken Wallis Hall, Norfolk and Suffolk Aviation Museum, Flixton, Bungay.

Note From the East Anglian Air Ambulance

Since its launch in 2000, the East Anglian Air Ambulance's (EAAA's) medically equipped aircraft with their highly skilled doctors and paramedics, have helped to save hundreds of lives and improved the outcomes of many other victims of accidents and medical emergencies across the region. It has achieved this despite receiving no direct government or National Lottery funding and has to raise over £3.5 million each year to sustain the service.

Operational 365 days a year, the EAAA funds two helicopters crewed by highly skilled doctors and paramedics. Anglia One serves Suffolk and Norfolk while Anglia Two serves Bedfordshire and Cambridgeshire. Their most frequent callouts are to the scenes of serious road traffic collisions, but falls and equestrian accidents are also regular missions, as are those to the scenes of industrial or agricultural accidents. Patients suffering medical emergencies, such as cardiac arrests or strokes, can benefit from the service particularly if they are in one of the region's many remote or inaccessible locations when the emergency occurs.

The combination of the aircrafts' speed and the expertise of their doctors and paramedics enables them to effectively bring the accident and emergency department to the accident site, starting definitive, potentially life-saving treatment within minutes of the incident. If necessary, patients can also be flown to the most suitable hospital in the region to treat their condition. In some cases, travelling by air means that patients can reach in minutes, a destination that could take over an hour by road.

Peter Gunn hopes to donate a percentage of the profits from his book *Flying Lives with a Norfolk Theme* to the EAAA and the charity is grateful to him for this generous gesture.

For more information about the EAAA and how you can support its vital work, contact the charity on 0845 066 9999 or visit its website at www.eaaa.org.uk.

We need you today. You may need us tomorrow.

Reg. Charity No. 1083876

BIBLIOGRAPHY

General Works

Burnett, John, *A History of the Cost of Living* (Penguin 1969)
Chronicle of Aviation *(JL International Publishing 1992)*
Elliott, Christopher, *Aeronauts and Aviators* (Terence Dalton Limited, Lavenham, Suffolk, 1971).
Fairhead, H., and Tuffen, R., *Norfolk Airfields and Airstrips* (Norfolk and Suffolk Aviation Museum 1988)
Holmes, Richard, *Redcoat* (HarperCollins*Publishers* 2001)
Pugh, Martin, *We Danced All Night: A Social History of Britain between the Wars* (Vintage Books London 2009)
Snowden Gamble, C. F., *The Story of a North Sea Air Station* (Neville Spearman Limited 1967).
Stevenson, John, *British Society 1914-45* (Penguin 1984)

Newspaper sources:
Eastern Daily Press archives (Norfolk Local Studies Library).

On line-sources:
The Times Digital Archive (via the Norfolk County Library website).
Oxford Dictionary of National Biography (via the Norfolk County Library website).
www.flightglobal.com   (*Flight* Magazine 1909-2005)
www.cwgc.org (Commonwealth War Graves Commission)

By chapter:

1. Balloon Mania and the Norfolk Connection
Archive sources:
Books:

Money, Major (later Lieutenant-General) John, *The History of the Campaign of 1792 between the Armies of France under Generals Dumourier, Valence etc. and the Allies under the Duke of Brunswick* (London 1794).
Rigby, Edward, *Account of Mr James Deeker's Two Aerial Expeditions from the City of Norwich – June 1785* (Norwich 1785).
Rush, George, *Accounts of Ascents of Nassau and Victoria Balloons 1838, 1849, and 1850* (London 1851).

Articles:
Townshend, Marquis, 'A Poetical Epistle on Major Money's Ascent in a Balloon from the City of Norwich and his Descent into the Sea'. (Norfolk Heritage Centre).

Money, Major (later Lieutenant-General) John, 'A Short Treatise on the use of Balloons and Field Observators in Military Operations', London 1803. (Norfolk Heritage Centre).

„   „   „   „   „   „   'Letter to the Right Hon. Wm. Windham on the Defence of the Country at the Present Crisis', Crown Point, Norwich May 20 1806. (Norfolk Heritage Centre).

Other sources:
Royal Aeronautical Society:
Major B. F. S. Baden-Powell Collection of aeronautical cuttings 1783-1904. (Royal Air Force Museum, Hendon).

General:
Barney, John, *The Defence of Norfolk 1793-1815: Norfolk in the Napoleonic Wars* (Mintaka Books Norwich 2000).
Carew, Tim, *The Royal Norfolk Regiment* (Famous Regiments Series: The Royal Norfolk Regiment Association 1991).
Hodgson, J. E., *The History of Aeronautics in Great Britain* (Oxford University Press 1924).
Paton-Williams, David, *Katterfelto, prince of puff* (Matador 2008).
Letcher, Piers, *Eccentric France: The Bradt Guide to Mad, Magical and Marvellous France* (Bradt Travel Guides Ltd UK 2003).
Mackie, Charles, *Norfolk Annals*, Vol I 1801-1850 (Compiled from *The Norfolk Chronicle*) (Norfolk Heritage Centre).
Martins, Susanna Wade, *A History of Norfolk* (Phillimore 1984).
Meeres, Frank, *History of Norwich* (Phillimore 1998).
Rolt, L. T. C., *The Balloonists: the History of the First Aeronauts* (Sutton Publishing Limited 2006).
Norfolk Chronicle & Norwich Gazette (1815).
Norwich Mercury, July 1785, February 1815.
Thetford & Watton Weekly Standard & Post (from 1912).
Lord, Jim, 'The remarkable John Money' Norwich News, *The Sedgwick Magazine*, March 1992. (Norfolk Heritage Centre).
Penny, John, *Ballooning in the Bristol region, 1784 to 1786*: the opening chapter in the History of Local Manned Flight. (Bristol Past: Fishponds Local History Society).

2. Charles Herbert Collet – Pioneer Marine Aviator
Archive sources:
Dulwich College, Roll of Honour, documents and notes, courtesy of Calista M. Lucy, Keeper of the Archives.
Southampton City Libraries, copies of letters and newspaper reports.

General:
Sturtivant, Ray, and Page, Gordon, *Royal Navy Aircraft Serials and Units 1911-1919* (Air-Britain 1992).
Warner, Philip, *The Best of British Pluck – The Boy's Own Paper revisited* (Book Club Associates London 1976).

'First long distance flight over West Norfolk' by Ray Wilson (The *Citizen* 14 November 1990).

3. The Darleys – Brother-in-Arms at War
Archive sources:
National Archives (NA):
- ADM 273/7 p61
- AIR 1/39
- AIR 1/43/15/9/17
- AIR 1/46/15/9/25
- AIR 27, No. 1089; App. 'A'; App. 'B'; App. 'C'.

RAF Museum, Hendon: Doc. DC 76/74/268.
Dulwich College, documents and notes, courtesy of Calista M. Lucy, Keeper of the Archives.

General:
Barker, Ralph, *The Royal Flying Corps in France* (Constable, London 1994)
Boyle, Andrew, *Trenchard, Man of Vision* (Collins 1962).
Insall, A. J., *Observer: Memoirs of the Royal Flying Corps 1915-18* (William Kimber & Co. Ltd 1970).
Jacklin, David, *'The Super Handley'* (privately published by D. Jacklin 2008).
Jones, H. A., *The War in the Air* Vol VI.
Steel, Nigel and Hart, Peter, *Tumult in the Clouds: The British Experience of the War in the Air 1914-1918* (Hodder and Stoughton 1997).
Wise, S. F., *Canadian Airmen and the First World War: The Official History of the Royal Canadian Air Force* Vol 1.
Eastern Daily Press, 'The last flight of a hero' by Steve Snelling, 23 November 2002.
Shrewsbury Chronicle, 3 October 1919.

4. Thomas Keppel North and the Vickers Vimy
Archive sources:
The Vickers Archive, University of Cambridge Library, Doc. Nos 621, 622, 623, 2345.

General:
Daniel, Peter, *A Magnificent Town and its Flying Machines* (London Borough of Bexley 2009).
Thetford, Owen, *Aircraft of the Royal Air Force since 1918* (Putnam 1988).
Thomas, E. O., *Crayford: A History* (London Borough of Bexley 2008).
Eastern Daily Press (EDP24), *Hidden Norfolk: Mystery behind air epic* 11 June 2005, by Tom North (nephew of Thomas Keppel North).
On-line sources:
BBC London, *Flying High in aviation history*, on-line reference.
www.kentrail.co.uk/vickers_crayford

5. Egbert Cadbury – Zeppelin Hunter
Eastern Daily Press, 'King of the Zeppelin Hunters' by Steve Snelling, 5 August 1998.

On-line source:
www.fengatesroad.com

6. G. S. M. Insall VC – War Hero and Pioneer of Aerial Archaeology

Deuel, Leo, *Flights into Yesterday: The Story of Aerial Archaeology* (Pelican Books 1973).
Hauser, Kitty, *Bloody Old Britain: O. G. S. Crawford and the Archaeology of Modern Life* (Granta Books, London 2008).
Insall, A. J., *Observer: Memoirs of the Royal Flying Corps 1915-18* (William Kimber & Co. Ltd 1970).
'How traces of history marked an aerial milestone', Steve Snelling (*Eastern Daily Press* Magazine 24 July 1999).
Joseph Helingoe – CD recording 25 March 1976 (RAF Museum).

7. Nevil Shute (Nevil Shute Norway) – Aeronautical Engineer and Novelist
Archive sources:
British Library: Nevil Shute Norway's correspondence with Society of Authors 1923-55 (Dept. of Manuscripts ref. Add MS 56763).

General:
Gunn, Peter B., *Bircham Newton: A Norfolk Airfield in War and Peace* (2002).
Gunn, Peter B., *Naught Escapes Us: The Story of No. 206 Squadron Royal Air Force* (The 206 Squadron Association 2004).
Price, Alfred, *Aircraft Versus Submarine* (Jane's 1980).
Shute, Nevil, *Slide Rule* (William Heinemann Ltd 1954, subsequent editions by Pan Books).
Shute, Nevil, *Landfall* (William Heinemann Ltd 1940, subsequent editions by Pan Books).
Sturtivant, Ray, *Anson File* (Air-Britain 1988).
Terraine, John, *Business in Great Waters: the U-Boat Wars 1916-1945* (Mandarin 1989).
'The Snapper Incident', by John Anderson (2007, Nevil Shute Foundation).
'The stammerer who lived to tell stories', by Philip Hensher (*Daily Telegraph* Review 5 December 2009)
On line source:
The Nevil Shute Norway Foundation at www.nevilshute.org

8. Alan Cobham and the Barnstormers, Joy-riders and Circus flyers
Cobham, Sir Alan, *A Time to Fly* (Shepheard-Walwyn (Publishers) Limited 1978).
Fahie, Michael, *A Harvest of Memories: The life of Pauline Gower MBE* (GMS Enterprises 1995).
Luff, David, *Mollison: The Flying Scotsman* (Smithsonian Institute, Washington 1993).
Notes from The 3rd Sir Alan J. Cobham Memorial Lecture, Sir Peter G. Masefield, delivered on 17 June 1982. (Royal Aeronautical Society Library).
The Citizen, article by Ray Wilson 9 August 1989, 'Barnard's Air Circus'.
Ibid. 18 October 1989 'Pre-war air displays at Heacham'.

9. Lawrence Edwards – The First Officer Prisoner of War

Brickhill, Paul, and Norton, Conrad, *Escape to Danger* (Faber and Faber Limited).

McNeill, Ross, *Royal Air Force Coastal Command Losses of the Second World War* Volume I 1939-41 (Midland Publishing 2003).

Rollings, Charles, *Prisoner of War: Voices from Behind the Wire in the Second World War* (Ebury Press 2007).

Rollings, Charles, *Wire and Walls: RAF Prisoners of War in Itzehoe, Spangenberg and Thorn 1939-42* (Ian Allan 2003).

Rollings, Charles, *Wire and Worse: RAF Prisoners of War in Laufen, Biberach, Lübeck and Warburg 1940-42* (Ian Allan 2004).

10. Basil Embry – Wartime Escaper and Great Air Commander

Embry, Air Chief Marshal Sir Basil, *Mission Completed* (Four Square Books 1958)

Richardson, Anthony, *Wingless Victory* (Pan Books 1965)

See also Reed, John (below).

11. Percy Charles Pickard – Bomber Pilot and Amiens Prison Raid Hero

Hamilton, Alexander, *Wings of Night: The Secret Missions of Group Captain Pickard DSO DFC* (Crécy Books Ltd 1993).

Orchard, Adrian, *Group Captain Charles "Pick" Pickard DSO**, DFC 1915-1944* (The Society of Old Framlinghamians February 2006).

Reed, John, *After the Battle* Journal, No. 28, 'Operation Jericho: the Amiens Raid'.

13. Wing Commander Ken Wallis – Norfolk's Very Own Flying Legend

Hancock, Ian, *The Lives of Ken Wallis: Engineer and Aviator Extraordinaire* (Ian Hancock, 5th ed.2010).

'Magnificent Ken and his Flying Machines' by Tom Walshe (*Eastern Daily Press* Sunday supplement 24 April 2010).

On-line sources:

www.gyroplanepassion.com

www.aviationmuseum.net

www.aeroventure.org.uk

INDEX

Note: Illustrations have *italic* page numbers.